The Bicycle Manual
on Maintenance and Repairs

The Bicycle Manual
on Maintenance and Repairs

ROBERT WHITER,
an associate of
the Incorporated
Institute of
Cycle Traders
and Repairers

Contemporary Books, Inc.
Chicago

Illustrations by Robert Whiter

Copyright © 1972 by Laurida Books Publishing Co.
All rights reserved
Published by arrangement with Laurida Books Publishing Co.
Manufactured in the United States of America
Library of Congress Catalog Card Number: 80-7484
International Standard Book Number: 0-8092-7136-2 (cloth)
0-8092-7135-4 (paper)

Contemporary Books, Inc.
180 North Michigan Avenue
Chicago, Illinois 60601

Published by arrangement with Laurida Books Publishing Co.
simultaneously in Canada by
Beaverbooks
953 Dillingham Road
Pickering, Ontario L1W 1Z7
Canada

CONTENTS

To the memory of

my revered mentor

Robert Putney,

whose bicycle frame-building genius gave me guidance and

inspiration when I was a young boy.

PREFACE

As a young boy in England, I became fascinated with the bicycle and entered the cycle trade as an apprentice frame-builder. After serving for almost thirty-five years as master repairman, shop foreman and shop owner, my love for bicycles has carried me into maturity and I am happy to tell you that I am still working at the thing I like best here in America.

Throughout the years I have eagerly searched for literature on the complex and mechanical world of bicycles in libraries and bookshops that would further enhance my knowledge, on both sides of the Atlantic. I regret to inform you that I have not had much luck finding books on the subject, and those that I did encounter touched but briefly on maintenance and repairs.

In this modern age of great technological advancement, the bicycle has kept-in-step and has become highly sophisticated with its multi-speed gearing and lightweight. Not since the last bike boom of the 1890's, when the automobile was invented, has there been such renewed world-wide interest in the bicycle. People have become disenchanted with the automobile which is the major cause of air-pollution in our cities. They are ecology-minded and have discovered the health benefits and physical fitness that the bicycle affords. The current bike boom that began in the 1970's promises to surpass in popularity the one of last century.

These are times when the entire bicycle industry is in a state of confusion because the demand for bikes and parts exceed their ability to supply. They are unable to train qualified mechanics and bicycle shops are ill-equipped to handle repairs.

It is because of this paucity of literature and the shortage of mechanics that I have written THE BICYCLE MANUAL. I sincerely hope you the reader; amateur or professional mechanic; bicycle enthusiasts and kids of all ages will learn and profit from my own personal and practical experiences.

Today more than ever does the ancient Latin maxim apply when purchasing bicycles, parts and repairs: *"Caveat Emptor"*.

Robert Whiter
Los Angeles, California

ANATOMY OF THE BICYCLE

BRAKE LEVERS

GOOSENECK

HEAD TUBE

FRONT BRAKE

TOP TUBE

GEAR LEVERS

FRONT FORK

FRONT HUB

SEAT

SEAT TUBE

FRONT CHANGER

DOWN TUBE

TOE CLIPS

SEAT POST

REAR BRAKE

CRANK

PEDALS

REAR DERAILLEUR

DOUBLE CHAIN WHEELS

FREEWHEEL CLUSTER

1

FRAMES, CONSTRUCTION, REPAIR AND ENAMELLING

The frame, by this of course, I mean the frame set, is the front fork together with the frame.

Whether your bicycle or the one you intend to purchase is a single-speed machine with a foot-brake (coaster or back-pedalling-brake) fitted with balloon or middleweight tires, a 3-speed lightweight with narrow wheels and two handbrakes, a touring 10-speed lightweight or a racing bike, the frame is the most important part of a bicycle.

There are so many cheap machines on the market produced domestically and abroad, that it is a wonder how many of them stay together.

Whatever you intend to use your bicycle for, make doubly sure the machine you buy has a well-built frame.

Getting down to basic facts, a bicycle frame consists of several pieces of steel tubing joined together to roughly form a diamond. This shape has proved itself to be the strongest design through the years.

Of utmost importance in frame construction are the places where the tubes join. These areas should be carefully checked by you.

There are various methods of frame construction.

Most of the American bicycle frames have the tubes butted up against each other and are held in position with a little brazing material that is run around the joints.

The troubles encountered with in this type of frame construction result from the fact that not nearly enough brass or bronze is used. Coupled with usage of poor quality steel, breakage frequently occurs.

On the other hand, when the frame is constructed with

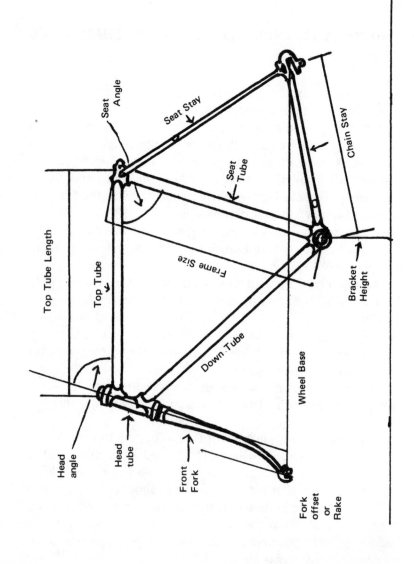

good quality steel and fillets of *bronze* (not brass) are carefully placed and run around all the joints, this will result in a strong responsive frame.

This latter method should not be confused with the resistance welding technique generally used only with tubing of greater thickness.

This kind of joint is of the fusion weld variety that causes the tubes to run into each other. In other words no brass or bronze is used whatsoever.

Although at first sight, this type of joint looks the same as the bronze welded kind, two points are different.

The first and foremost is weight—any type of steel welding relies on penetration—thus necessitating thicker gauge tubing.

Secondly, in the resistance weld the joining area of the head and top and down tubes generally occurs about an inch from the head on top and down tubes. (See illustration.)

This can be felt by the hand if not visible to the naked eye. This type of frame is nearly always constructed from one inch tubing as opposed to 1 inch top tube, 1-1/8 inch down and top tubes.

Most of the European bicycle frames are lug constructed. Lugs are pressed or cast tubular joints into which the frame tubes proper are brazed or in some cases silver-soldered.

On cheaper frames the lugs appear thick and clumsy.

On middle class types a slight tapering and cut-away is apparent.

On higher grade machines the lugs are delicately tapered, filed and cut away to a large extent, sometimes most artistically.

The reasons for the differences are as follows: The thick clumsy lugs with no cut-away parts are a lot easier and quicker to braze together in the cheaper grades.

The medium grade is a little more difficult. But as both these grades are generally dip-brazed in order to speed production it is of little consequence.

The higher grade frames are usually hearth-brazed by hand

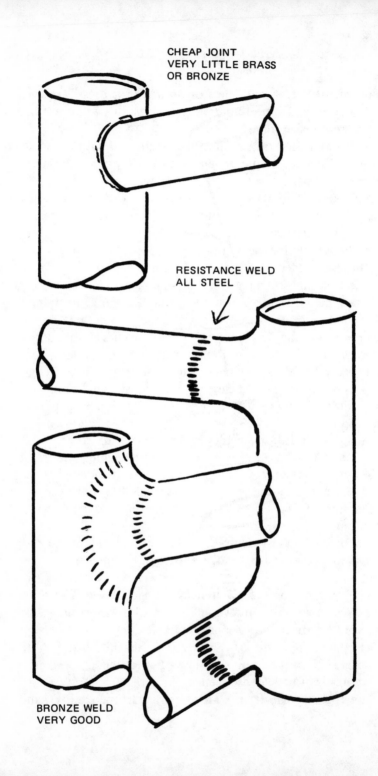

CHEAP JOINT
VERY LITTLE BRASS
OR BRONZE

RESISTANCE WELD
ALL STEEL

BRONZE WELD
VERY GOOD

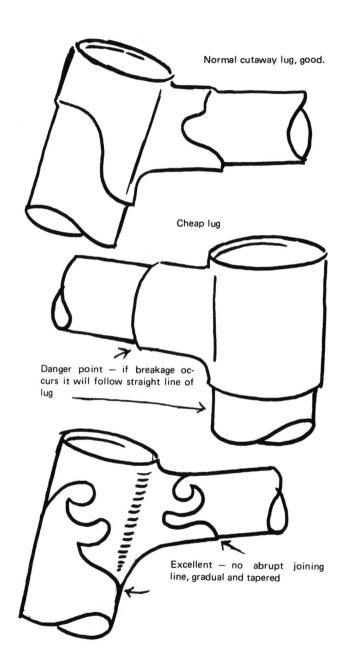

Normal cutaway lug, good.

Cheap lug

Danger point — if breakage occurs it will follow straight line of lug

Excellent — no abrupt joining line, gradual and tapered

and require not a little skill to keep the dividing line—where outline of lug meets tube free from brass.

One often reads that the lug frame is the strongest. But this statement can bear close scrutiny.

As a frame builder with almost thirty-five years of experience I would say this: A lug can hide a multitude of sins. The strength of a frame lies in the point where tube meets tube. These should be mitred and fit perfectly.

I have noticed in many frames that I have repaired while putting in new tubes, top and down, those gaps in the lug which were not apparent from the outside.

In these cases there was just the thickness or thinness of the lug holding the frame together. This results in a very weak frame that creates a good percentage of whip!

On the other hand, a good bronze welded frame where the tubes have been mitred perfectly, where a good fillet of bronze has been run around the joint and then carefully filed is as strong as any lugged frame.

Paradoxically, reverting to lugs correctly done, the more wavy the edges and the more it is tapered down (apart from lightening purposes) the stronger will be the joint.

In other words, the demarcation line of the two thicknesses of metal should be gradual and spread over as large an area as possible. This again will be apparent in a first class bronze-welded joint.

Another advantage in the bronze-welded process is that the frame can be built to almost any specification, whereas in the lugged frame one is governed by the set angles of the lugs.

Lug pulling is practiced by some frame builders to alter the angles, but beyond the change of just a few degrees this is not desirable.

Speaking of angles, back in the thirties, small frames with very sloping head and seat angles were all the rage. Gradually these angles began to change from the 69 degree head to 73 degrees which gave a more upright machine.

It must be understood, however, that even though an up-

Example of plain cut away head lugs and fork crown.

Example of fancy cut away head lugs and fork crown.

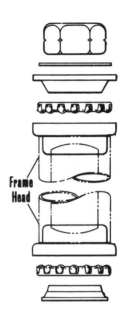

Frame
Head

Example of American type head showing balls in cages.

Italian frame head lugs and seat cluster

right design makes for a responsive bicycle, too steep a head will create fatigue for the rider over long distances.

Thus for road work in touring or racing a compromise is generally reached—a 72 degree parallel frame with both head and seat at 72 degrees.

For track racing over short distances we go back to steep head angles and even surpass them with 74 degree and 75 degree heads. These are quite common today.

In relation to the frame angles we have the wheel base. Upright angles allow for a short wheel base, whereas shallow angles tend to increase the length of the wheel base.

It should be noted that other things have to be taken into consideration.

The frame size is measured from the center of the bottom-bracket axle to the top of the seat cluster. A tall rider will naturally require a large frame—unless he has a short reach—he will need a length of top tube comparable to the height of the seat tube. This will make the front of the frame larger than is normal.

However, the rear triangle composed of seat and chain stays can to some extent be shortened accordingly.

This is commonly referred to as a "short back." Various methods have been tried in order to obtain ultra-short wheel bases.

In the thirties the Saxon Cycle Co. used twin seat tubes so that the rear wheel could be brought forward further with the result that the tire was almost between the two tubes. Another method has been to use a curved seat tube, but this idea seems to have been relegated these days to tandems.

While we are on the subject of the rear end, road bicycles are usually built with diagonal dropouts; track machines have the openings to the rear and are known as track ends.

It should also be observed that machines built for touring have mudguards or fender eyes incorporated in the dropouts, whereas those that are equipped with track ends have these omitted.

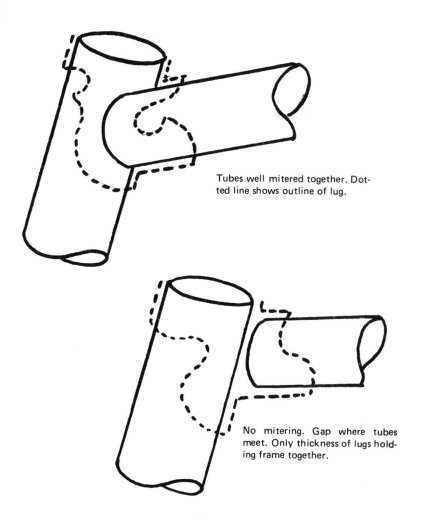

Tubes well mitered together. Dotted line shows outline of lug.

No mitering. Gap where tubes meet. Only thickness of lugs holding frame together.

The front fork is very important and should have the correct *offset* or *rake* in relation to the head angle. If this is not observed, the top tube of the bicycle will rise and fall when the front wheel is turned, instead of remaining parallel to the ground.

For roadwork, a nice gradual curve is desirable. This should give the bicycle resilience and help to iron out the road shocks. Speed with comfort is the goal for this type of machine.

But in company with the super upright design of the track machine a much straighter fork is used, and once more the absence of fender eyes will be noticed.

We have already referred briefly to the thickness of frame tubing when the method of resistance welding is used to unite the tubes together.

Incidentally, some frames will be found where the actual joints have been steel or fusion welded.

A good example is the Italian "Hermes" bicycle where the welding was left rough and not filed.

But as we have previously noted, in any form steel welding depends on penetration; so that the tubing has to be of a thicker gauge.

This is fine where weight is not the consideration, but if we wish for a really lightweight bicycle we have to start with a light frame. Therefore, we must use light tubing in its construction.

One of the oldest brand names in the business of bicycling, of course, is Reynolds. I have in my possession copies of cycling magazines from 1909 advertising this firm's butted tubing.

However, it was not until the middle thirties that we first heard of the celebrated mark 531.

So important was the introduction of this most important "improvement" to the bicycle, that the Cyclist's Touring Club of Great Britain awarded the makers their special plaque.

Illustration from advertisement in 1909
entitled
Reynolds Butted Tube
Name of Firm
"The Patent Butted Tube Co., Ltd."

Accles and Pollack is another company famous for light weight tubing, in this case Chrome Molybdenum. Both firms I understand are now controlled by Tube Investments Co.

These two types of tubing are excellent material and will be found in most of the top grade frames.

The 531 transfer or decal will be found in various designations and sizes and should be carefully studied when you are buying a frame or a complete bicycle.

One sees many advertisements for machines built with 531 Reynold's tubing—but this does not always mean what it says—so be sure to look at the decal.

This is generally found on the seat tube just below the seat lug cluster. One decal will say "frame tubes of 531," this means seat stays; chain stays and front fork blades are *not* 531.

Another will say "plain gauge 531 tubes," but the decal we are really interested in will specifically say, "built with Reynold's 531 butted frame tubes, forks and stays."

I should mention at this juncture a word about "double butted": This means that the tubing is not of the same gauge its entire length, but rather it is thin in the middle, gradually increasing in thickness as it approaches the ends. (See illustration.)

The outside diameter, however, remains constant the entire length of the tube.

This factor coupled with the manganese-molybdenum alloy steel content of 531 has proved to be very successful.

Not only does it give greater all-around strength and resistance to fatigue, but when the frame builder uses the correct brazing temperature—unlike cheaper grade tubing—531 retains almost all of its high tensile strength. This will especially occur where the joints of the frame are brazed.

Other makes of tubing found in good quality bicycles include the following: Columbus, Durifort and Vitus.

Some of the most widely used makes of lugs today are produced by the French firm of "Nervex."

Only the Top Tube. Seat Tube, and Down Tube of a frame with this transfer are made from REYNOLDS 531 Tubing—Plain Gauge.

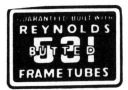

The same three tubes are REYNOLDS 531 when the frame bears this transfer, but this time they are BUTTED.

All the tubing in a bicycle with this transfer is REYNOLDS 531 — Frame Tubes. Chain and Seat Stays and Fork Blades, and it is all plain gauge tubing.

This transfer signifies that the bicycle is an aristocrat, a thorough-bred — made throughout of REYNOLDS 531 Tubing. BUTTED for Lightness with Strength.

SEE PAGE 54 FOR OTHER REYNOLD'S TRANSFERS

Their best pattern is the "Professional" followed by the *"Serie Legere."* We have here good design combined with lightness and strength.

Most lugs and fork crowns are "pressed out" as opposed to the older form of castings. Again this makes for greater lightness and will reduce the amount of filing required.

Some frame builders obtain their lugs "blank" and cut out their own designs. This raises the price of the completed frame or bicycle considerably and is generally restricted to special orders from customers.

I remember the case of an Indian Rajah who ordered a custom built bicycle for his son. He demanded the workmanship and finish to be so intricate that the lugs alone took one year to be cut out and filed, and when finished the lugs were inlaid with gold.

Some other well-known lug sets are made by Brampton, Chater-Lea, Bocama, Eklar and Prugnat.

Prugnat is setting the trend for Italian frame styling which is so popular at this moment.

When you are considering buying a used bicycle, particular attention should be paid to the top and down tubes.

Specifically, where they joint the head tube.

These areas, together with the front fork, are most likely to show damage if the bicycle has been in an accident of the "head on variety."

If this has occured and the bike frame tubes took most of the impact, this will be apparent in the form of "puckers" or "ripples" on the top and creases underneath.

Even if the impact was slight and the damage is not noticeable to the layman, a blistering of the paint is nearly always visible which will indicate that the metal has endured some stress or strain.

When the used bicycle is a cheap make it is not worth buying under the above conditions. If the price asked for is very low, it might be a good buy, however, as the remainder of the bicycle could be used for spare parts.

On the other hand, if the bicycle is of a better quality, it might be worthwhile considering buying but only at a low price. If the frame is in really good condition, you should be able to have two new tubes brazed into it.

When the tubes are only slightly bent and rippled, it is possible to straighten them.

To do this we need a good strong bench fitted with a vise.

A steel rod approximately 1-1/8 inch thick and long enough, so that when mounted vertically in the vise with the cycle framehead tube placed over it, it protrudes for about an inch, assuming that the cycle has already had the front fork, wheel and handle bars removed. (See instruction section on dismantling.)

Always leave the head ball cups in place. This will prevent distortion of the head tube when tension is brought to bear.

Invert the frame when placing it on the steel rod. (Note)

As we will have to use quite an amount of downward pressure, it is a good plan to prop a piece of stout timber or a length of steel under the vise overhang, with the other end resting on the floor.

Now, grasping the rear triangle, near the rear dropouts, assert a downward pressure in a steady manner. No jerks, please!

If you can get a friend to help you, have him watch the bent area as you pull. In this way you will not over do it.

When you are satisfied that the frame tubes are as straight as possible, examine them carefully for "crystalization."

If necessary, remove the paint for this purpose.

If a grey stretched look presents itself, this can be dangerous. *You should never use a frame that is in this condition.*

If you have no doubt whatsoever that the frame is worth saving, either get two new tubes installed or cut the head and sleeve it. (See section on "sleeving" later on.)

Any small dents you find can be filled in with solder.

Please remember that "cleanliness" is the key note in any form of soldering.

Using emery cloth alone is not enough. The entire surrounding area should be scraped with a pen knife, and be
careful not to touch it with the naked fingers.

Use a large iron, again, remember that cleanliness is most
important.

The tip should be cleaned, (use an old file for this purpose)
and then tin it.

Run some liquid flux into the dent. If in paste form use a
small piece of wood to apply. (A child's popsicle stick is
ideal.)

After the iron has been heated and dipped in flux touch
the tip with the solder stick so that a coating of solder forms.
Do not be afraid to build the solder up and overlap the dent.
The important thing is to get the work heated in a uniform
manner so that the solder flows over the whole area. Avoid
applying the solder in dribs and drabs, otherwise you will
find it could flake off when you come to dress it down.

Using an old file being careful not to file into the tube, file
down the solder until smooth with the tube and finish off
with a strip of emery cloth. If you are using an electric iron,
you will not have to worry about constant heat. But if you
have to do the job with a gas or blow torch heated iron, do
not try to finish with an underheated tool. If you have a lot
of dents to fill, it is a good idea to have two irons going.
While you are using one, the other can be on top of the blow
torch heating up and ready to be used as soon as the other
one cools off. This is known as "tinning" the iron.

Now rub the iron over the dented part a few times.

If your cleaning was carried out correctly, you should be
able to transfer some of the solder from the iron to the tube.

While keeping the iron resting on the work you should
then use the end of your solder stick.

As we are using the solder merely as a filler, and strength
is not the pertinent factor, it is quite proper to use resin
cored solder.

At this point it is important to remember that although we

have straightened the head, the frame could still be out of track.

In this case, the head tube when viewed from the front, could be out of line with the seat tube.

But before we attempt to rectify this, it should be clearly understood that we must make sure the rest of the frame is also in track. To do this correctly it is necessary to have the frame completely disassembled.

This step in tracking a frame is to insure that both seat tube and down tube are at right angles to the bracket-shell.

This should not be confused with the angle of seat and down tubes when frame is viewed from the side.

With the bracket cups out, lay a straight edge across the face of the bracket shell in line with and in the middle of the seat tube.

Get your friend, using a ruler, to take two or three readings inside of straight edge to outside of tube. One near the bracket, one halfway up, and one just below the seat cluster.

These should all be equal. If the readings increase near to the top, this means the tube has to be pulled over until the measurements conform with each other.

To do this, clamp the bracket shell in the vise making sure you have the jaws protected with aluminum or copper.

A gradual controlled pull has to be cultivated and do not be discouraged should you need to have the frame in and out of the vise to check several times.

Do not become impatient! When you have this in line, follow the same procedure with the down tube.

Finally, for the front diamond we must sight through the head and seat to insure that they are dead-in-line.

It will assist you here if you use a sighting board. This can consist of a large sheet of paper pinned on the wall and, together with good lighting you will be able to see any discrepancy.

To clinch the matter, slide one end of the straight edge through the head tube which should be in a horizontal position. With one hand on each side grasping the straight edge, push it against the inside of the head tube.

If you have the ball cups in place make a two point contact.

Now you have a greater sighting radius, as you can run your eye along the length of the straight edge, gradually focussing it in relation to the seat tube.

If the head is crooked to the seat tube, we use our old friend the steel rod again.

This time, however, we clamp it horizontally in the vise, leaving enough sticking out for the head tube to slide over.

With the rest of the frame vertical, that is—rear ends will be on top—we grasp the frame in one hand by the bottom bracket hanger while the other hand grasps it at the seat cluster.

We now impart a twisting motion turning in the direction that will bring the head tube in line with the seat tube.

Once again, exercise caution and patience.

The frame should now be placed in the vise, the jaws gripping it on each side of the bottom-bracket hanger.

We need the straight edge again.

This is placed through the frame as follows: One end rests against the head tube, edgewise; the middle part against the seat tube so that the other end will be approximately adjacent to the rear fork ends.

Have your friend measure the distance from the edge of the straightedge to the other side of the frame, again checking the inside measurement.

They should be equal. Most frames are built with a 4-1/2 inch clearance between the rear ends, but as hubs do and can vary, check your rear wheel cone measurement, before working on the rear triangle.

If the two measurements do not tally, grip the dropout of the side that is in too far. And with firm but controlled pressure pull out and check with straight edge.

The other seat and chain stay normally (in relation to the

side just corrected) would be out too far, so we pull this part in, using the same technique and checking with the straight edge.

Assuming your rear wheel is perfectly dished and true, it can be used as a finishing touch to assure ourselves that it runs central in the frame.

Check the distances on both sides of the rim at the junction of the seat stay and chain stay bridges.

If either the seat or chain stays are bent or dented, this should be attended to before tracking. Dents can be filled in with solder. (See previous notes on soldering.)

To straighten bends in the seat stays, make up two pieces of wood about two inches wide, about one inch thick and approximately four inches in length.

With the aid of a rat-tail file (round tapered) file a groove in the middle of the wide part, but running lengthwise.

On both pieces this should conform to the diameter and shape of the frame member.

Placing the bent part of the stay with your two templates on either side in the vise, you will find that with a gradual tightening of the vise handle you can straighten your stay accordingly.

Caution should be used here. Otherwise you will crush the member which after all is merely a tapered tube.

In extreme cases you may have to resort to resting the stay on a flat surface, bent part uppermost. And using a single block of wood with a groove filed in the end, you can then tap it out with a hammer, checking frequently with a straight edge.

A similar procedure can be carried out with a bent chain stay.

After straightening a really bad bend in either of the seat stays, hold the frame upside down and place a spare rear axle in the drop outs.

Now rest a set square across the chain stays as near to the bracket shell as possible and sight. Both top of square and axle should be dead-in-line.

While we have the frame dismantled, it is a good idea to check it thoroughly to make sure all the brazed joints are secure.

Special attention should be paid to the rear dropouts.

Sometimes insufficient brass or bronze was used which would cause the ends to come loose.

The same thing applies to the tops of the seat stays where they are fastened to the seat lug cluster.

Make sure both seat and chain stay bridges are secure.

How about the brake hole in the bridge? Is it distorted or crushed? If it is flattened, it can be restored to its former round shape with careful manipulation of the vise grips.

Make a note that when the brake is reinstalled to use the correct seating pads.

If the hole is enlarged or distorted, I would suggest making up a bushing.

This would be in the form of a steel tube with the inside diameter just large enough to go over the brake bolt.

If the only tubing you can find is too large, cut a piece out lengthwise and form it around the brake bolt.

Next, enlarge the hole in the bridge, using either a reamer, a rat-tail file or a correct size drill taking care to keep the hole at the proper angle in relation to the seat stay which is usually at right angles.

The sleeve should be a push fit and then brazed in place and filed flush.

You will now have a nice rigid mounting for your rear brake. (See caliper brakes and adjustment.)

Regarding brazing, you will have to take it to a shop if you are an ordinary cyclist.

But if you are working in a shop we can assume the workshop will have brazing or welding equipment.

Repairs to frames should never be welded in the sense of using steel filler rod as used in fusion welding.

If you have a broken frame tube, do not take it to the nearest car service station. Chances are the man there will just pick up his torch and fusion weld it. Unless he is a very experienced welder the weld will not be successful.

As we have mentioned previously, this type of welding demands thickness of material for penetration.

Broken tubes should be cleaned on the inside and a sleeve made up which should fit nice and snug.

The ends of the sleeve should not be left straight but should be made wavy and rather like a cutaway lug in reverse.

Before inserting the sleeve it should be fluxed, the "Borax" mixed with water and daubed on.

Whenever possible try to get equal lengths of the sleeve in each of the broken parts.

In order to get the sleeve in, it is generally necessary to gently spring the two fractured pieces apart.

When in place it should be "pinned" by drilling a 1/16" hole on each side of the break—preferably not in line—and plugging the holes with tapered pins. But as long as it is mild steel, any form of pin will suffice.

For best results the part to be brazed should be laid on a hearth which consists of a steel box open on one side containing a lining of bricks.

Use genuine fire bricks if available, otherwise ordinary house bricks, broken up, will make a fairly good substitute.

Make sure some of the bricks are grouped about the part you wish to braze.

If you do not have a proper brazing torch, you can use the oxyacetylene torch, putting on the largest tip.

Work of this kind requires a deep soaking heat as opposed to the local pencil type flame used in welding.

The trick is to get the work a uniform cherry red, at which time you should just touch the crack or break with the brass rod when it will flow right around the joint and penetrate both sides of the sleeve.

When doing this make sure the pins get brazed in. The reason for the pins, by the way, is not so much for strength but to make sure the two pieces do not move while being brazed.

As you are aware, metal will expand when heated. It should be noted when using the oxyacetylene torch because of the different flame content, it is advisable to keep the flame moving so as not to get the work too hot.

We have spoken on frames at some length and we should now consider the front fork especially when damaged in an accident.

This usually comes under the category of our old friend the "head on" which results in bending the "blades" back.

If the impact is severe the column or steering tube will also get bent.

We are then faced with the question of whether the fork can be straightened, and if so will it be safe?

Raleigh's service department in England used to state they would straighten a column on its own or they would straighten the blades, but they would not do both.

In other words, it was time for a new fork. In my own opinion, if you have any doubt, install a new one.

Before proceeding we should mention another cause for fork damage.

Lightweight generators which incorporate the head lamp such as JOS and Soubitez are very popular.

As these bolt on to the left fork blade it is very important to insure that lock washers are used and that the 3 bolts are checked regularly.

If this is not carried out, there is a possibility, because of vibration, that the generator will loosen up and drop down and swing into the wheel.

The results are easily visualized. But to get back to straightening, the first thing to do is to check the column for straightness.

If the tube is distorted, the actual bend will be apparent by the shine caused by rubbing against the inside of the head tube.

To be straightened the column must be held in the vise securely. In order not to crush the tube we have to follow one of two procedures.

The first procedure is the use of specially shaped vise jaws, flat on the outside to match the vise, concave on the inside to fit around the tube.

The second is the fitting of a steel mandril inside the column.

If we adopt the first method, the column is placed in the protector with the end approximately flush with the bend. This assembly is then clamped in the vise so that the bend is horizontal.

A steel mandril (the end of which must be small enough) is then inserted into the bottom of the fork crown.

This mandril should be about 8 inches long.

To get maximum leverage, we use a length of steel pipe which fits over the mandril.

Now, by exerting pressure on the pipe we can straighten the column.

As we have already stated in previous discussions on straightening, proceed with caution. Do not be in a hurry!

You may find after the initial operation that it is necessary to slide the column along a little way as the bend at times is spread over a fairly large area.

Constant checking with the square is a must. Use it for testing all round straightness of the column and also to insure that it is at right angles with the fork crown.

The handle end should be laid alongside the column with the blade part crossing at right angles.

Gradually slide the square towards the crown until the edge is level. You will be able to see whether or not the crown is at right angles to the column.

The Y shaped piece rests on the bend which is nearly

always situated close to the crown.

With gentle exertion pull on the handle and keep your eye at all times on the blade.

We do not want to pull the blade too far forward as this could put a ripple in it.

When you believe that you have it straight, turn the fork over and follow the same procedure.

If you do not have access to a fork straightener, you can in an emergency use both hands—simply pulling the blade in the right direction.

You will notice in our discussions on both frame and fork bending we have not mentioned using heat. We feel that in most cases the bend can be best straightened cold.

Using heat presents many problems for the novice bicycle mechanic; such as creating too much heat which can cause the tubing to dent in or ripple when the work has tension put on it. (As in the case of straightening.)

In the case of fork alignment, it will be found in the majority of times that when both blades are bent they go back together. So much, in fact, that many people after seeing a bent fork think that it is in the correct shape.

This brings us to a novel tool you can make up, if you are not concerned too much about perfect accuracy.

Find a piece of steel pipe approximately 2 feet in length and about 1-1/2 inches in diameter of a good substantial gauge.

Get two pieces of flat steel about 3 inches by 1-1/2 inches and roughly 1/8-inch thick.

Bolt one piece across one end of the steel pipe to form a T and the other about 6 inches away.

All you now have to do is clamp the fork in the vise as you would to straighten the blades separately.

But in this case the T goes across both of the blades where the bend is. The other piece also goes across but farther behind with the pipe running through the middle of the blades.

You will find that you now have a powerful lever, which with care, will pull both of the blades into line.

Whatever method you use, the next step is to check that both blades are equal.

Grip the column lightly in the vise with the crown horizontal and the offset upwards.

Place a straight front axle in the fork ends and then place your square across the blades adjacent to the crown.

Get down to eye level and sight the axle across the top of the square. They should be parallel.

If they are not, slide the square towards the axle. In this way you can usually find where the variance is.

When you find the spot, mark it.

Turn the fork around in the vise until it is in the position you originally had it for straightening, and pull the offending blade into line.

Check again with the axle and square until equal.

The thing we have to be sure of before the fork is ready to be re-installed, is accuracy sideways.

Place the fork in the vise with the crown horizontal.

You need a small straightedge, the width of which should be just wide enough to fit in the top of the vise on top of the fork column.

Place it so that it extends between the dropouts. You will now be able to measure the distance each dropout is away from the straightedge.

Most forks are built to a standard 3-1/2 inch opening, but some hubs do vary.

So check your front hub cone measurement. If the blades are out, pull them into the correct alignment and with the right distance between the ends.

Final check: Make sure your front wheel is true and lined dead center over the outside lock nuts.

Install it, minus tire and tube in your front fork.

Check to see whether it is perfectly in the center and lock it up tight with the outer nuts.

Now take the long straightedge and lay it edgewise across the wheel so that it rests on two places on the rim.

Holding it firmly in place, let the long end swing over towards the column. There should be a very small space between straightedge and the end of column.

Turn over the straightedge and do the same thing to the other side. The spaces should be equal. If they are not, recheck your column and crown.

Remember, they should be at right angles and then recheck the angle of the blades in relation to the column sideway.

We mentioned previously the possibility of having two new tubes brazed in the "punched up" frame.

The first thing is to procure some tubing.

531 tubing is not always easy to get hold of, assuming the frame was originally built of this high grade product.

Good quality molybdenum tubing can generally be obtained from a good hardware store.

We will need two lengths, the down tube 1-1/8", approximately 26 inches long, and the top tube 1 inch diameter approximately 24 inches in length.

I say approximately because the lengths vary with the size of the frame; so measure the existing tubes allowing for the bends, and also some extra for the mitring.

Make sure the tubing is "cold drawn and seamless."

If there is any doubt whether the tubes are seamed, just look through them into the light.

When measuring tube lengths remember that—with the exception of the actual frame size which is measured from the center of bottom-bracket hanger to top of the seat cluster bolt—the others are measured center to center.

For example, if we wish to find the length of the top tube, we take a point in the middle of the head tube, in line with the middle, horizontally of the top tube.

Next, following this line we take it to the middle of the seat cluster. The distance between these two points is the length of the top tube.

Similarly, if we take a point from the middle of the head tube again, but this time at the lower head lug and follow a line down to the middle of the bottom-bracket hanger, the distance between these two points is the length of the down tube.

Reverting to tubing for the moment, we should mention that it might not be possible to get this double butted anywhere but from a recognized bicycle wholesaler.

If forced to go to a hardware store, try to get it in a decent gauge, 22 would be suitable.

After all when going to the trouble of repairing a lightweight frame, there is no point in putting heavy gauge tubing in it.

Next, find out whether the lugs are pinned. Most of the good quality hand built frames are pinned, but do not be too surprised if yours is not.

Some of the cheaper grade frames have spot welded lugs and others merely center punch the lug with the indentation going through to the tube.

If pins are present, the one at the bottom-bracket hanger is usually easy to find—simply put your finger in the housing and up the down tube.

When you find it on the inside, check where the head is on the outside.

To do this, lightly file around the area, it will appear as a small circle of gold. Using a center punch, carefully pop it in the middle.

Select a drill the same size and then drill it out. The object is to keep the drill straight (it will require a little practice to drill on tubing, as the bit tends to keyhole instead of making a nice clean circular hole).

The other three places will not be so easy to find. The first thing is to file the remaining lugs.

The pin should be on the underside where the lug pattern is normally left larger than the rest of the design.

From time to time hold the frame so that the light is falling on the lug in question.

Now rotate it. In most cases this should show you where it is.

Sometimes the pressure holes, these are holes drilled in the tube, correspond with the end of the adjoining tube.

For example, if you take out the seat post from a bicycle and look into the seat cluster, where the top tube joins it, you should see a hole. This hole is there to allow an escape for the pressure which would otherwise build up when the brazing is carried out.

Sometimes this hole is small and will not be much use to us, but if it is of a fair size we can shine a flash light into it and often see the pin.

The same thing applies to the two head joining areas; however, as the down tube has an opening at the bottom where it joins the bracket assembly, frame builders do not always trouble to put a hole in the bottom head lug position.

It should be mentioned that it is not uncommon for manufacturers to put two pins in lugs; one on each side.

The idea here is that one pin will not influence the joint and pull the tube out of alignment.

But getting back to finding the pins, as a last resort, we have to cut at least one of the tubes in half to unbraze them.

Once again we can use our old standby, the flash light. Shine it down the tube from the cut portion and we should be able to see the pin or pins location!

But let us be positive about this. *Do not* attempt to unbraze until absolutely certain we have all the pins cleanly drilled out.

The normal procedure is to cut the top tube in half and unbraze the bottom tube from the bottom-bracket shell. Obviously, if we have a proper brazing torch, this is the tool to use.

Place the frame in the hearth with the bricks accentuated around the bracket.

Have an open container of Borax (brazing flux) and a spatula handy because sometimes a stubborn joint can be assisted to become unbrazed with the introduction of some flux.

Grasp the head of the frame with the left hand and after lighting the torch direct the flame to the bracket, making sure that the heat is going to the lug and not the tube.

In any form of brazing or welding always direct the flame to the thickest part as the pieces that need to be joined or separated might be of unequal thickness.

What we should aim for is soaking heat—so do not be in a hurry!

When the joint is of a uniform cherry red, very gently attempt to twist the head—if nothing happens prolong the heating and then try again.

If still stubborn, dip the spatula in the flux and deposit it on the outer edge of the lug so that the flux runs in.

All this time we are keeping the heat constant and at the same time being careful not to scorch the tube.

A common failing is for a practice to occur which leaves a broken piece of the tube in the lug.

Try the twisting motion again. Experience will tell you when it is ready.

Gently pull the tube out with a twisting motion until completely clear of the lug.

As we have cut the top tube, we do not have as much to hold on to.

And in order not to burn our hand, we select a short piece of thick tubing of the right diameter that will fit in the cut end of the top tube.

With the use of the vise grips we clamp hold of this end. The use of a liner will be readily understood as the thin gauge top tube would collapse under the pressure of the vise grips.

Follow the same method as for the bracket procedure; likewise, for the two head joints.

If we are not fortunate enough to have a proper brazing

torch, it is possible to do the job with the oxyacetylene welding kit, as long as we use a large tip.

Here we have to be more careful because the flame is so much more intense and we will probably find that we will have to chase the heat, while keeping the flame rotating around the lug.

In these cases you may find it easier to clamp the hanger bracket in the vise when unbrazing, likewise when separating the head unions, a solid rod horizontally clamped in the vise over which we can then slip the head tube.

It will be found in these circumstances that the rod is best when nearly the same diameter as the inside of the head tube.

Again it will be found advantageous to use the liner and vise grip method. Let us again stress the importance of patience and gentleness when attempting to pull the tubing out.

Next step is to lay the unbrazed pieces of tubing out on the bench and check the lengths against our previous measurements which should have been written down and pinned up for ready reference.

Now examine the ends where they were brazed and inspect the mitring.

If good you can use this as a pattern for your new tubing. Do this with a hack saw and half-round file, being positive you know which end is which, as if the head and seat angles were not parallel, the mitring will vary.

Also be careful to maintain the correct length. It is very easy to take pains over the mitre on each end and then find you have made the tube too long.

Of course, this will only mean that you have to do your work over again.

The real bugbear is to find you have too short a tube. Do not forget that particularly with the top tube the largest cutaway of the mitre does not occur on the same side of the tube.

When convinced that the mitring and lengths are identical

to the old tubes, inspect the lugs.

In some cases it will be found that you will have to ream them out slightly. This is because a thin coating of brass has been left inside, or if you had the misfortune of having a tube break off inside, this too, will have to be removed.

Any stubborn pieces can be dislodged with the use of a rotary grinding stone bit installed in the electric pistol type drill.

Care must be taken not to take too much out and to keep the inside perfectly round. Remember, always, that good brazing depends a lot on a nice tight fit.

This is accomplished by constant trial and error. The ends of the tubes should be cleaned with emery cloth.

The best way is with the tube clamped in the vise (do not forget to use your jaw protectors and exercise care not to overtighten).

The emery is then torn into strips and with an end in each hand is pulled up and down over the tube. The tube is rotated as each part becomes bright.

When you have 4 nice fitting joints and are satisfied the mitring allows the end of each tube to butt up tight against its opposite number, you should drill into the tubes using the existing holes in the lugs as guides.

Next, lightly pin all 4 joints. Note: In order to get the old pins out, you may have had to drill an oversize hole; so a larger pin is the answer, unless the taper of the pins allows for a greater tolerance.

If you do not have a frame building jig, use the following routine: Clear a space either on the bench or a clean space on the floor.

If you have floor boards you can use one of the joining cracks as your base line.

Measure up 13-1/2 inches from this line and draw a parallel line (I am assuming that you have 27 inch wheels).

Slip the fork with the head fittings into the head. Do not worry about the ball-bearings at this stage.

Gently lay the frame and fork on the floor so that the drawn line runs through the middle of the front fork dropout and through the middle of the rear dropout slot (this is generally located immediately under the seat stay).

Bottom-bracket heights with 27-inch wheels are in the majority of cases 11 inches, with 26-inch wheels 10-1/2 inches. So check this by measuring center of bracket shell to ground line.

You now have the all important factor. Measure from the ground line to top of top tube near the seat lug. Move across and take another reading near the head tube, making the second measurement parallel to the first. They should tally!

This means that the top tube will be parallel to the ground.

Finally, make sure you have not slipped up anywhere, see how much clearance you have between middle of bracket and front fork end.

The best way is to rest the crank with pedal on the bracket in the position it would normally be with crank horizontal.

Now install front wheel with tire in the front fork and allow for toe-clips. There should be clearance when the front wheel is turned. The actual distance of course depends on the original design of the frame.

Having reassured ourselves that all is in order, we take out the fork and pull the frame apart.

With some Borax mixed with water to form a paste, we coat the end of the tubes, re-install them and hammer in the pins.

With our straightedge we track the frame (see previous notes on this operation) and starting with the bracket shell we commence brazing.

Once again, play the flame on the lug rather than the tube, and get the work a uniform cherry red.

Keeping the heat constant, touch your brazing wire—which should be dipped in the flux—onto the edge of the lug.

If your heat is correct the brass should literally be swallowed up by the lug. Care must be taken not to fill up any intricate patterns or cut-outs of the lug.

Should you be unlucky and overload the lug, you should have a steel brush handy and with the flame still going brush off the surplus.

Please be sure the brass, bronze or silver solder—depending on the medium used—penetrates to the closed end of the lug.

As mentioned previously this is where the real strength lies.

While your lugs are cooling off and you are using a smaller tip of oxyacetylene torch, you can braze on any lever bosses, cable eyes, pump pegs, etc. that were on the old tubing or any new braze-on bits that you now want on your frame.

Many times even the well-known manufacturers put the top tube cable eye too far back making too tight a curve on the brake cable—now you have the chance to rectify this, if your bicycle is equipped with center-pull brakes, but the cable adjuster bracket was fastened on by the seat bolt—a most unsatisfactory arrangement.

How about making and brazing on a subsidiary bridge for this purpose and then you do not have to worry when adjusting your seat height whether or not you are upsetting your brake adjustment.

All you need is a strip of mild steel approximately 1/4-inch wide, 1/16-inch thick and approximately 3-1/2 inches long.

Form this into a U Shape, making sure both legs are equal. Drill a 3/16-inch hole dead-in-the-middle and there you are.

Scrape off the old paint on each seat stay and braze in place. Depending on your frame size allow for the "throw" of your brake when marking position for brazing.

Note that on some frames this might not be possible. This is the reason you may have seen some bicycles, with center-pull front and side-pull rear.

If you are artistic, you can with a round-file dress the straight lines of your bracket and put a little finesse to it.

Our lugs have now cooled off and we can proceed to file

them using a round, half-round and pillar file.

Carefully follow the contours of the lug noting not to allow the file to slip and dig into the tubing.

Any of the glass-like substances (hardened flux) can be gently tapped off and routed out of the cutaway with the corner of the file.

Finish off with the emery strips, again keeping the material moving so as not to get any flats and to keep the graduation of the lugs even.

Next, carefully file and finish with emery any other brazed-on bits.

This can all be hard work for you, but with patience and care the finished article can be very rewarding.

Naturally, you will want to recheck to see that the frame—after all this—is still in track. One more thing still has to be done, as we now have a frame with some parts painted and other parts with exposed steel.

Obviously it cannot be left like this. It does not look right and if the steel is left in this condition it is going to rust; therefore, it must be painted.

Bicycle frames when new are either sprayed or dipped in enamel and then stoved in an oven until they have a glass-hard finish.

Unless we have access to this method or know of a firm close by that does stove enamelling, we will have to do the job ourselves.

Patience and care is also called for here and can result in your getting a first rate finish.

First to consider is the removal of all the old paint, and this can be carried out in a variety of ways.

If you have a sand blaster handy either in your workshop or in the vicinity, you will have several points in your favor.

Not only will it take off the old paint but if you have the frame blasted before you file off the lugs, it will also take off any surplus brass and flux.

This will usually clean up the lugs and make less work for

you in finishing off.

Lastly it will give the frame an overall matt finish with thousands of minute indentations and provide a key for the enamel to cling to.

The next step calls for using paint stripper and this idea I do not like.

If the original enamel is of a good quality it takes a long time to penetrate and make the part soft enough to be able to scrape off.

Even then it is a messy job and one must be very careful to neutralize it before repainting.

Nothing is more frustrating than when getting a nice finish on a frame, only to have the paint start to bubble around some crevice where the stripper sank in and you were not able to offset its chemical action.

This will boil down to judicious usage of the blow torch and wire brush—particularly effective around the joints and awkward places.

The main tubes and seat and chain stays will present none or very few problems.

When you have done all you can with the torch and brush, give it a good rubbing with coarse emery, finishing off with fine.

If you have an erecting stand, put a seat pillar in the frame and in turn hold this member in the erector. Another method is to hang the frame from the ceiling.

After having used the emery do not touch the frame with your hands.

I even like to wash the frame with hot water and detergent, rinsing off and drying with a clean rag.

It is important that all grease is eliminated from the surface of the tubing.

Using a Red Oxide undercoat (Schwinn produces some excellent bicycle spray paint) go all over the frame and fork getting a nice even coat, going for the awkward to get at places and any braze-on fitments first.

The important thing with all spray paint is to thoroughly shake up the can, get the ball inside really rattling! Hold the can 10 to 12 inches away from the work for best results.

Let it really dry (patience is the watchword). While waiting, you can make up your mind as to what finish, color etc., that you want.

Do you want any panels or bands such as a different color on the seat tube? If you do, it is best to put these on first.

Let us assume that we are going to color the frame a flamboyant blue with a 6-inch white band on the seat tube. With the undercoat dry we check it to make sure there are no runs, lumps or roughspots.

If these are present they can be gently rubbed down either with very fine emery or fine steel wool and then carefully sprayed again.

When this is completely dry, take a can of white and spray the middle of the seat tube fading off and overlapping the 6-inch length we originally decided on.

Do this with several coats of fine spray, letting each coat dry thoroughly.

The final coat should be put on wet but at the same time avoiding runs.

At this stage it is a good idea for you to find something else to do, such as, cleaning the bottom-bracket and head cups and bearings, getting them ready for reassembling in the frame.

In this way we forget about the frame momentarily and give the paint a good chance to dry.

When certain that the white is dry, get a sheet of white paper about 5-3/4" long and wide enough to go around the frame tube and overlap itself.

Secure this with masking tape, sealing it lengthwise and overlapping top and bottom to the overall length of 6 inches.

While on the subject of masking, perhaps I should have mentioned earlier that if your front and rear fork ends are chromed, you should mask them off before commencing to

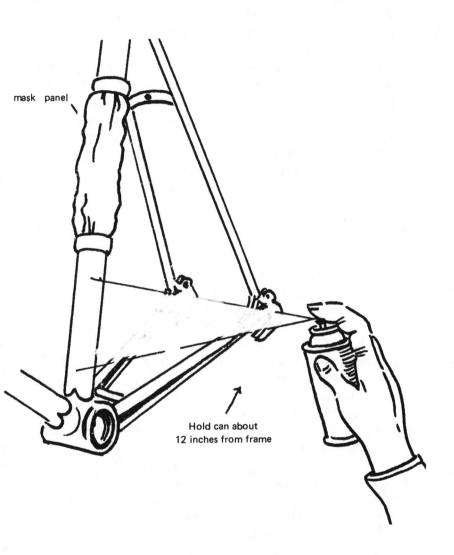

mask panel

Hold can about
12 inches from frame

spray the frame.

You can either wrap the ends with paper and hold it in place and finish off the demarcation line with masking tape or simply wrap the chrome part with the tape in the same way you would tape a handlebar.

Getting back to painting, we now have to put on the silver undercoat. With a flamboyant finish the top coat is semitransparent which allows the silver to shine through.

The other metallic finish is known as Polychromatic or more commonly lustre or metal flake. In this coating the actual color has aluminum flakes mixed with it.

In the old days the flamboyant finishes had the frame nickel plated instead of a silver painted undercoat. The finished paint job really had a lustrous look.

Today nickeling would really increase prices, so we have to make do with silver paint.

Once again shake the can well up and down and start spraying, doing the awkward places first.

Put on a light coat and let dry, finishing up with a nice flowing coat—you will realize that it is important to get this coat nice and smooth, so that the last coat and finish look their best.

Let this silver coat really dry and harden before applying the blue finishing coat.

It should be noted that during all spraying it is important to keep the paint well-mixed by frequently shaking the can.

Another good tip is to keep the nozzle clean by wiping from time to time.

Be very careful when applying the color coat to go all over lightly at first and then build up gradually keeping the same depth of color. Nothing looks worse than parts of the frame that are dark while other parts are distinctly lighter.

When you are satisfied you have a nice uniform coating let it dry, and then and only then, carefully peel off the masking. If you are doing it for yourself, the rest is up to you. If it is for a customer he will tell you how he wants it finished.

You can finish the white panel off with either tricolor or olympic bands should the edges (despite your careful placing of the masking tape) look uneven.

If you have a steady hand you can outline the lugs.

Here the secret is in a good brush and having the paint mixed to the right consistency.

A good tip here is to keep a rag handy that is lightly dipped in lacquer thinner, so that if you make a mistake you can wipe it off before it dries.

Decals or transfers, when you have the right ones to match the make, carefully applied can really put a fine finish to a frame.

These come in three styles.

First we have the spirit fixing type, in my opinion still the best. To apply, pull off the protecting tissue and then coat the actual decal—and nothing else—with metholated spirit or rubbing alcohol.

Allow it to almost dry before applying to the frame. Be careful to place them on the actual spot the first time, as once on it is not easy to shift them.

Now rub the back with the handle of a spoon and wait for about 15 minutes; then you can remove the backing by saturating it in water, lightly wipe off the surplus water with a sponge and then let dry.

The second type is the well known water slide off variety.

These are simply floated in water, preferably luke warm (should the decals be a little old, cold water will crack them).

As soon as you see them start to lift, take them out and gently slide them through your fingers to remove the surplus water.

Apply the decal face side up, sliding it from the backing onto the frame.

With this type you have the chance to move them around should you not be satisfied with the first placing.

The third and latest type resembles the first. The main difference is that the decal is already coated with a tacky substance. Otherwise you can follow the same directions.

One word of warning: If you are thinking of spraying your finished frame with a protective coat of clear lacquer, try it out on a separate piece first. Most colors come in lacquer and enamel.

So be on the safe side and use each coat of the same pattern.

Do not mix lacquer with enamel. Most enamels will go over lacquer, while most lacquers will lift or cause enamel to bubble.

This is the same with decals. So unless you can obtain clear enamel do not chance it.

The alternative is to use a good quality clear varnish and this way you can be sure of not spoiling the decals.

Make sure that you obtain a decent brush, one that does not start shedding hairs, and apply with long, flowing strokes.

Your finished article should be nice and smooth and free from brush marks.

Unless you have a steady hand and the correct brush do not try lining or pinstriping the frame (a lining brush has very long bristles 3/4 of which length are laid on the frame and drawn along producing a uniform line).

Today lining boxes seem to have ousted the brush.

This set-up consists of a small, serrated, spring-loaded wheel resting in a slot at the bottom of a container which is filled with paint.

As the wheel rotates it transfers the paint to the frame giving a thin and steady line.

It is usually fitted with a guide that cuts out the worry of keeping the hand steady.

Therefore, should you really want to line your frame get hold of a lining box.

2

FRONT FORK, DISMANTLING AND REASSEMBLING

The first step is to remove the handle bars. We do this first because if tight, we can put the front wheel between our legs and thus have some leverage.

When we say tight, we naturally do not mean when the gooseneck is "frozen" in the fork column.

This requires sterner methods of removal and we do not suggest you ruin your front wheel in the process.

Most handlebars and goosenecks today are found held in place with an expander bolt.

To remove you simply unscrew the hex head which is found on the top until it protrudes about a quarter of an inch.

Then with a block of wood between give it a smart tap with a hammer. Providing that the gooseneck is not corroded, you will find you will be able to remove the handlebar assembly with a twisting and pulling motion.

If the bicycle is equipped with cable brakes, you can disconnect these in several ways depending on the reason for dismantling the head.

If you wish to leave your brake bottom parts on and retain the adjustment, carry out the following if of the Weinman side pull brake type.

Unscrew the small nut that holds the adjusting assembly to the brake, pull away the adjuster unit and replace the nut.

By doing this you will get plenty of cable slack enabling you to slip the nipple end out of the lever.

This procedure can be carried out with levers that have a slotted nipple socket.

With center-pull brakes squeeze the blocks together and

SECTION ON FRONT FORK
SHOWING: – COLUMN OR STEERING TUBE

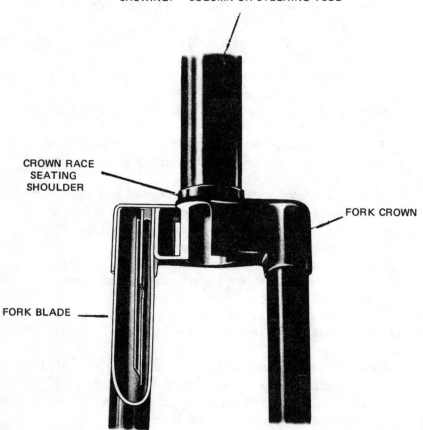

CROWN RACE
SEATING
SHOULDER

FORK CROWN

FORK BLADE

CAMPAGNOLO STRADA
HEAD SET

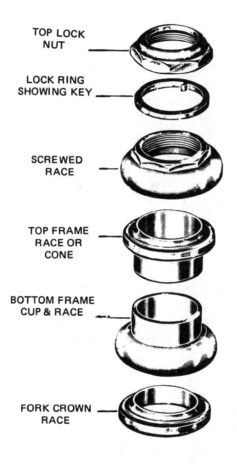

TOP LOCK
NUT

LOCK RING
SHOWING KEY

SCREWED
RACE

TOP FRAME
RACE OR
CONE

BOTTOM FRAME
CUP & RACE

FORK CROWN
RACE

remove the subsidiary cable.

If the brake blocks are adjusted too close for you to do this, loosen one of them and lower or remove completely. If fitted with quick-release, simply flip the lever. This will automatically cause the brake blocks to open wider.

If you wish to remove the brakes completely, simply undo the nut at the rear of the fork crown for front brake, and the nut to the front of the seat bridge for rear brake. There are exceptions. (See further discussion of brakes.)

But returning to the head, if you are unlucky and come across a really stubborn gooseneck, try and run some penetrating oil down between the gooseneck and fork column.

Do this from the top and then turn the bicycle upside down and pour some in from the fork crown end.

If you do not have some penetrating oil such as "liquid wrench," W.D. 40 can be very useful.

Let it soak for awhile and then give the gooseneck a good tapping all over with a rubber mallet.

Now try to turn it. If it still will not move it is time for sterner methods.

Get a block of wood, a piece of 2 x 4 will suit the purpose, and rest one end under the extension part of the gooseneck. With your friend holding onto the front fork, give it a few hard hits with a hammer. This should do the trick.

Sometimes you will find that the cone or expander lug which is connected to the bolt has become rusted or corroded within the fork.

In this case the best remedy is to unscrew and remove the bolt completely.

You will usually find that it is now possible to remove the gooseneck.

This will leave the cone in the fork and with the gooseneck out of the fork, screw the expander bolt back into the cone.

With an old pair of vise grips, especially kept for such work, place them under the hex head and clamp securely.

Now you can with the use of the hammer, strike the vise

grip from underneath as near as possible to the bolt.

This should set it loose.

If not, invert the frame and with a stout steel rod knock out the cone or lug from the bottom of the fork.

Note that we are speaking of forks that have an open column at the bottom.

In some American forks which have a closed bottom, you can only use the previous removal methods.

We now come to the head bearings.

These we refer to as the head set.

In the past there was a different method of clamping the handlebars (and some of these can still be found). This type of fitting is known as the head clip. This served two purposes.

One as already stated. The other as a combined upper head race and additional lock for the head.

This consists of a ball-bearing holder or race but different than the normal screwed head race, in that it is not threaded.

Integral with this race is a short piece of tubing, the upper part of which is split and has provisions for a nut and bolt held horizontally.

A normal head lock-nut completed the set.

For this arrangement to work satisfactorily, the fork column itself had to be cut or slotted.

The pattern of the cutting resembled an old crossbow.

In order to obtain adjustment the top nut would have to be tightened down until all play was taken out of the head.

While the handlebars were set in the required position, one had always to make sure that the bottom of the gooseneck was well below the bottom of the head clip. And then the headclip bolt had to be tightened until the handlebars were secure.

What actually happened here was that when tightened, the headclip compressed the fork column at the slotted part which in turn gripped the gooseneck.

One disadvantage with this type of headset was that it was

Because so many present day manufacturers are cashing in on the famous Reynold's hallmark it became necessary for them to embellish their transfer by adding the address of the company at the bottom.

By doing this there is now no doubt as to whether the frame is built of the genuine article.

Notice also the extra lightweight 531 transfer and Reynold's latest tubing 753 which is 50% stronger than 531 but still incredibly light. This tubing was used by Roy Schuiten in the World 5000 Meter Pursuit Championship when he won the "Grand Prize of Nations".

a little on the bulky side and because of its height did not allow the handlebars to be lowered as much as with the more conventional pattern. We should point out that the Raleigh company some years ago issued a composite head set on some of their more expensive models.

This set consisted of the customary screwed race but between it and the top lock-nut was a separate clip.

Here you would have a finer adjustment inasmuch as you could screw down the screwed race until all play was taken out of the head; and with the top nut tightened down after the handle bars were put in their correct position, the clip bolt would be tightened.

It should be pointed out that in both cases it is permissable to use goosenecks fitted with expander bolts.

To remove the front fork from the frame, it will be very helpful to have an erecting stand.

You will then be able to hold the bicycle in any position that you desire.

If you do not have an erecting stand you can hang the machine from the rafters.

Or as a last resort, you can lay the bicycle on the floor with a rag or cloth spread under the head. This is to enable you to catch any balls if you are dismantling any of a variety of European bicycles which usually have loose balls.

Today, however, many of these machines will have the balls in cages.

Two examples come to mind: Campagnolo headsets and the newest Peugeots are made with at least one of the head cups filled with a ball retainer.

We now return to dismantling.

With a large adjustable wrench or the Schwinn Special head wrench undo the top lock nut.

If it is a different style, domed and slotted, use a C spanner or wrench.

With these latter tools it is sometimes necessary to use a little persuasion in the form of a hammer and punch.

(Make a special blunt punch that fits the slots or use a copper or brass drift punch.

If the head set is of the expander bolt type, the next thing to do is remove the lock-washer (there is a type of Japanese head set that does not use one).

Some washers are merely that, simply washers, but generally they serve as a lock.

The most popular form has a pip sticking out on the inside that engages in a slot or groove contained in the fork column.

The other type has a D interior shape, the flat of which spot corresponds to the flat found in the column.

The object in both of these patterns is that they can only slide up or down on the fork but cannot rotate.

If the bicycle is fitted with center-pull brakes, an additional washer in the form of the cable hanger may be found. Follow the same directions for removing as for the lock-washer.

As an added security measure, some of these lock rings are serrated on the bottom to match the top of the screwed race or cone underneath.

The Peugeot bicycle uses a peg type.

The peg fits into one of a series of holes. As this is not visible or apparent until removed, care must be exercised when being removed.

When you are taking off the screwed race, have the bicycle upside down.

To remove, grip the race (if circular use a pair of VAR head pliers—if hex, use a large adjustable) and then unscrew the fork out of the race.

Carefully lift the fork out of the frame so as not to disturb the balls (assuming they are loose).

If you are doing the job without a stand, lay the frame flat on the floor—and as previously mentioned—spread a cloth under the head. This will stop any balls that drop out from bouncing away.

Wash out all cups, races and cones in kerosene. Follow this

with a good scrubbing of all the bearing surfaces. Slight wear if even is O.K. But any parts that are pitted should be replaced.

Likewise, if you should lose a ball or two, always replace the lot, otherwise the movement could be uneven.

When replacing the head fittings, always make sure the crown race is really tight on the fork crown.

If loose, even when installing a new one, here are a couple of remedies.

First clean up the circular shoulder on which the race fits.

Tin it with solder and then with a strip of tin plate also tinned, wind it around the shoulder and solder it in place.

Use this method when the race fits very loosely.

Otherwise, put a series of cuts around the shoulder with a small cold chisel raising up the surface in the process.

The race should be installed with a small amount of force, using a thick gauge piece of tubing which fits over the column.

This, when tapped down on top of the race gives an all around pressure.

When buying or fitting replacements there are several things to remember. First and foremost is the thread on the fork column.

These days fork columns have 1 inch outer diameters and mostly 24 threads per inch. This includes most American, British and Japanese bicycles, and many bicycles from other countries that are found in the United States.

There are some exceptions.

The Raleigh forks are threaded 26 T.P.I., while the Peugeot has mostly 25 T.P.I.

Among the Italian made bicycles which are generally threaded 25.4 x 24, it is likely that you will find some 24 T.P.I. threaded.

The Austrian Steyr is another bicycle that you must watch out for when replacing fork parts.

Make sure that they are exactly the same pattern.

V4 COMPETITION DESIGN

HEAD FITTING SETS

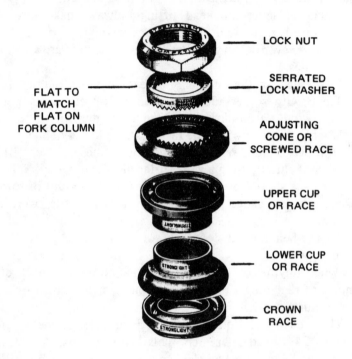

LOCK NUT

SERRATED LOCK WASHER

FLAT TO MATCH FLAT ON FORK COLUMN

ADJUSTING CONE OR SCREWED RACE

UPPER CUP OR RACE

LOWER CUP OR RACE

CROWN RACE

As we previously stated, some head sets use balls in cages or in retainers while others take loose balls. Some old British made bicycles may still be found, as the Phillips Dunelt brand which used 1/8-inch balls, 30 in number for the top, and 30 for the bottom.

Another difference is that the cups are separate from the seatings.

In even older models it will be found that the head race seatings are integral with the frame, being part and parcel, as it were, with the head lugs.

But most headsets today will be found with 5/32" balls, some as in most American bicycles in retainers and some loose.

The latter usually 25 top and 25 bottom.

But you should never take it for granted. Always count the balls when you take them out as there are many different types and patterns now in use.

It should also be noted that some head sets feature a cup and cone arrangement while in others they just have cups.

The Schwinn Bicycle Co. uses two distinct head sets on their machines.

Although both use the cone and cup system, there is a difference.

The lower cup and cone on both are interchangeable, but when we come to the upper pieces, herein lies the difference.

On the Schwinn Sting-Ray models, they use the same cup, top and bottom. The screwed race in this case is in the shape of a cone.

Whereas, in their Varsity and Continental models (to name just two), the upper frame race is the cone and the screwed race is like an inverted cup.

Both of these sets take balls in cages.

Be careful when you are replacing these retainers to install them correctly.

The cone has to engage the balls on the inside; the curved outer face of the retainer goes into the cup first.

With a good many ball cups, such as the Raleigh for example, the head set cups are not the same; the larger one always goes on the bottom.

If you have to remove the cups or race seatings, use a steel tube just smaller than the inside diameter of the head tube.

Push it down until the end engages with the lip of the cup and give a series of taps moving all around to give equal pressure.

Examine the balls for flats, pits or any other signs of wear.

Personally, with the relatively low cost of balls, I usually replace them anyway.

Inspect, carefully, the cups and cones.

A small amount of wear is permissible, just so long as it is even; but if there are any pits, cracks, etc., do not hesitate to replace them.

Returning to balls, for the moment, I know of some people who lose for example, 2 or 3 balls while removing the head set and they will replace just these missing ones with new balls. This is a bad practice.

The old balls must be slightly smaller than the new ones.

So, replacing some new, and using the rest of the old bearings makes for uneven adjustments; replace with all new balls.

Returning to the older head clip type of fitting, for an instant, always exercise care when you remove or replace this component.

Even when the bolt is loosened it will still fit snugly on the column.

Therefore, it is a good tip for you to pry the slotted section apart with a screw driver.

In so doing we stand less chance of spoiling the thread or catching the clip in the upper horizontal cut on the column.

The latter, especially, has to be avoided, as it could open this cut and thus bend the top of the column.

When replacing head fittings of the ball cage variety, it is a simple matter to do this with the frame in the normal vertical position.

As we have already mentioned, make sure the crown race is seated correctly and dead-tight on the crown.

Smear some grease in the frame cup or cups, depending on whether you have twin cups or a cone and cup set.

Slip the bottom ball cage over the column (see previous remarks on correct installation of retainer) and insert it up into the head tube.

If fitted with top cup, drop the ball cage in and lower the screwed race on to it.

If a frame cone, place the cage on top, followed by the screwed race, in this case filled with grease.

Hold the screwed race stationary, and as the top of the column meets it, automatically rotate the fork thus engaging the threads and keep turning until all play is taken up.

Replace the lock washer or any other in between pieces.

If the machine is fitted with center-pull brakes there will be a hanger or adjuster supporter.

With the Schwinn twin-stik levers there will be a bracket. The final stage will be in the installation of the top lock-nut.

At this juncture I do not completely tighten down. I reserve this job for the final adjustment when the machine is completely assembled.

To do this put the front brake on and place your hand on the junction of the lower ball cup and crown race.

Now try to rock the head. If you feel play, try tightening the head.

Repeat the test with the upper cup assembly. If after tightening, there is still play, this means either the crown race is loose or the race seatings are not seated correctly in the frame, so check accordingly.

3

BOTTOM BRACKET HANGER, CRANKS AND PEDALS

The bottom bracket hanger has been referred to as the engine room of the bicycle.

Call it what you will it is a very important part of the bicycle.

Situated at the bottom and junction of the seat and down tubes of the frame—not forgetting the seat stays—it has to be a rigid member; apart from housing the crank axle, it controls the rigidity of the whole frame to a great extent.

There are two main types: The one piece crank and the three piece crank.

Most American-made bicycles utilize the one piece crank.

As its name implies, it is in one piece—in other words both cranks and axle pivot are all in one.

Roughly shaped in the form of the letter Z, it passes right through the bracket housing and is held in place with cones threaded on to the axle part; these in turn engage bearings in cups pressed into the hanger.

There are several things to be taken into consideration when adjusting, overhauling or replacing any parts in this type of bracket.

If the crank is loose and just needs adjusting—remember the lefthand side is the adjusting side; in other words, the side opposite to the chain.

With a suitable wrench, a 12-inch crescent type will usually fit the bill, unscrew the hex nut. This has a left hand thread, therefore it unscrews to the right.

Under it you will find a lock washer. This will either cover the cone and have a half circular slot which will enable you

SECTION OF BOTTOM BRACKET HANGER
SHOWING: — INSIDE LINERS
SOMETIMES USED TO STRENGTHEN THE JOINTS

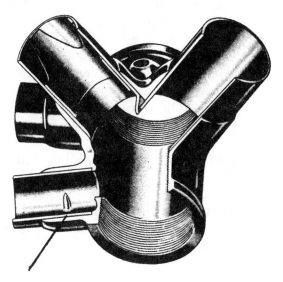

NOTE: BRAZING PEG.

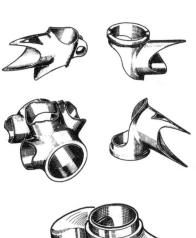

**NERVEX
PROFESSIONAL
SERIES LUG SET WAS
USED BY THEVENET
ON HIS PEUGEOT
WHEN HE WAS THE
WINNER OF THE 1975
TOUR DE FRANCE**

Nervex

to locate and tighten the adjusting cone, or it will be small enough to display the cone with a larger flange fitted with a groove which again will enable you to adjust it. This latter pattern is favored by the Schwinn company.

If, however, the bracket needs a complete overhaul, we must first of all remove the lefthand pedal; this unscrews to the right, or if you like, to the rear of the bicycle.

I do not think it will be amiss here if we mention a few facts about pedals.

A good rule to follow: One piece cranks take pedals with 1/2" x 20 T.P.I. This will depend again on whether they are rat-trap racing pedals or of the rubber type.

Right hand pedals that are marked with an R.(The French are marked D. for droit) screw in the crank to the right or to the front of the bicycle.

Left hand pedals marked L.(French G. for gauche)screw in to the left or again to the front of the bicycle when viewed from the left.

A word of warning. Some French cranks which appear to be 9/16" are actually a shallower thread and unless you have the correct replacement pedals you will have to tap out the thread to standard size.

Pedals should be checked quite frequently for tightness.

So many cranks are ruined unnecessarily by cyclists riding with loose pedals.

What generally happens is that the bicycle falls over and the pedal takes a lot of the shock, sticking out as they do makes them vulnerable.

This loosens the pedal and when ridden starts a see-sawing action, gradually stripping out the thread.

Therefore, when checking a bicycle do not forget to put the wrench on the pedals and make sure that they are tight.

Returning to the crank overhaul, after removing the left hand pedal, remove the hex nut, lock washer and cone, sliding them over the left arm of the crank.

AMERICAN ONE PIECE CRANK AND FITTINGS

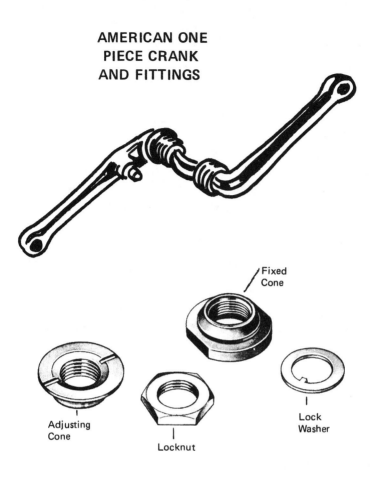

Fixed Cone

Adjusting Cone

Locknut

Lock Washer

Bottom Bracket Hanger Cup

Remove the ball retainer with a joggling action, and carefully remove the crank.

You will find the right hand cone screwed up against the sprocket; some models will be found with a spacing washer.

Examine both cones, cups and ball retainers—and if pitted, replace.

The right hand cone has a right hand thread; when replacing this component, be sure to tighten it up securely.

Failure to do this may result in a worn center hole in the sprocket, causing slippage eventually, particularly if the machine is of the coaster-brake type.

If parts need replacing, be careful to get the correct threads, ball and cup sizes.

Let us imagine that we have to replace the crank, due perhaps to stripped pedal threads. (If you do not have another crank, it is possible to retap to the larger size of 9/16", but this takes time and it is generally cheaper to replace.)

First of all, check the length of the cranks.

Next, check the cone threads of the crank; these will either be 24 T.P.I. or 28 T.P.I.

As we have stated, also check the cones for wear—if they have to be replaced, make sure, apart from having the right threads that they are the right shape; that is, the face of the cone which engages the balls is either a straight taper or has a concave radius.

Also check for depth—we have already mentioned spacing washers—if the cones we are using are deeper overall, place them on the bench side by side with the old cones together with their washers.

You can now see which washers to leave off when replacing—often you will find that you do not have to use any.

The ball retainers and cups also come in two sizes. Check these carefully as both types of cup fit in the bracket housing.

Although different manufacturers will be found using various code numbers, they are known as 64 and 66, many can still be found marked this way.

You will find when replacing the crank on some bicycles that the tolerance is very limited and that you will have to leave the left hand cup out until you have the crank located.

Do not forget the "golden rule" with ball retainers—fit them so the number and manufacturer's name is facing outward.

Above all, make sure you smear the cups with a good quality grease, and when making the final adjustment have the cranks so that they revolve freely without any shake or side play.

In case there is any doubt, I had better mention that the cups in this type of bracket are push fit; to remove, simply place a blunt drift punch, preferably of a soft nature, through one side of the bracket so that it rests against the inside of the opposite cup and tap out—and of course simply reverse the procedure for the other cup.

When replacing cups just tap them back in by using a copper or lead mallet.

Or you may use a tool consisting of two pieces of steel shaped to fit into the cups; these are drilled through the middle, a threaded rod passes through both holes.

This rod has a nut on each side which when tightened draw the cups into the bracket and seats them correctly.

The three-piece crank set-up comes in two main types, the cottered kind and the cotterless pattern.

Let us look at the cottered pattern:

This consists of an axle which depends on its shape and cut aways for installation and performance, there are no threads.

By shape we mean two circular shoulders, the outside acting as cones and engaging balls running in cups; these cups screw into the bracket shell.

The right hand cup generally has a flange or an interruption of the thread on the face side so that it can be locked

BOTTOM BRACKET
AXLES CRANKS
PINS

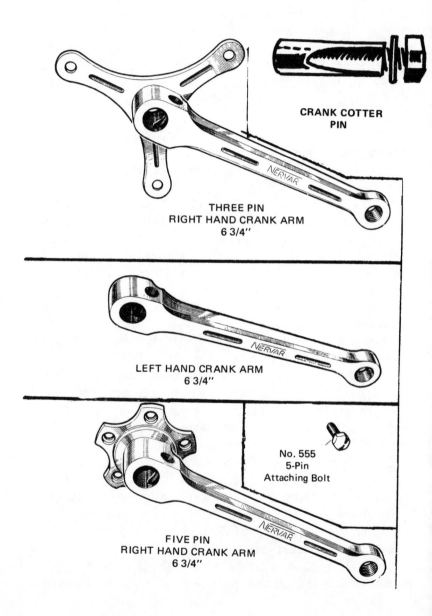

CRANK COTTER PIN

THREE PIN RIGHT HAND CRANK ARM 6 3/4"

LEFT HAND CRANK ARM 6 3/4"

No. 555
5-Pin
Attaching Bolt

FIVE PIN RIGHT HAND CRANK ARM 6 3/4"

tight against the frame.

When Raleigh uses their standard cup, they swage the metal from the bracket, over the cup, locking it securely; this swaging has to be removed if we wish to take out the cup.

The right hand side should have a left hand thread to help counteract the tendency for this cup to unscrew; most British built frames have this.

The Austrian Steyr bicycle also adopts this policy; but you should always check for yourself.

Many of the Italian and French frames have a right hand thread.

I suspect the reason for this is that when threading the bottom-bracket, it is easier to use just the one thread on both sides rather than to change over taps.

Before we move on from this very important part of the bracket, we should metnion a little trick if you have a persistent loosening of the cup.

Taking the cup out, carefully clean the threads of both cup and bracket with lacquer thinner and dry them off.

Now get some old paint, smear the threads of both cup and bracket well (naturally you will first mix the paint to get it to the proper consistency).

Screw the cup back into the frame using the bracket tool and lock up tight. It is important to let the paint set and dry hard before assembling the rest of the bracket set.

The tool consists of a piece of steel contoured to fit inside the cup and is drilled to permit a bolt to pass through and thread into an outer piece shaped to fit over the outer part of the cup, and is further equipped with two handles.

By using this tool you can readily tighten or loosen the right hand cup.

If you do not possess this tool—here is another tip—select a wrench that will fit the flats on the flange of the cup or as in some cases, a raised bar in the middle of the cup face.

Now here is the trick: if you try and use the wrench on its own, you will find that it keeps jumping off so find a bolt, the stouter the better just so long as it will go through the hole in the cup.

Under the head of the bolt place a thick washer—this end goes inside the cup and sticks out through the hole.

Now we need another washer or strip of steel large enough to go across the jaws of the wrench.

Finally, place a nut on the bolt and tighten down.

The result accomplished is that we have the wrench locked onto the cup, allowing us to use all the force we need to tighten or loosen the right hand cup without fear of it slipping off.

Of course, some cups will have notches on the outside of the flange or indentations on the cup face.

In this case we can either use a punch or again the aforementioned cup tool, using the peg variation instead of the normal flats on the flange attachment.

Returning to the right hand cup that persists in coming loose—here is a further tip to assist in keeping it tight—gently peen over the metal from the bracket onto one of the flats of the cup or center punch the metal to engage in one of the notches if so equipped.

Turn the frame upside down to do this so that it will not look unsightly.

But before we do all this we have to dismantle the bracket; we will have to remove the cranks which are held in place with tapered threaded pins, known as cottered pins.

Split keeper pins are sometimes called cotterpins, but in the bicycle trade cotter pins are solid and used in conjunction with cranks.

Cotter pins come in two main sizes, standard and continental, the latter are the thinner.

We are speaking of diameters, by the way, not the depths of the flats on the pins.

The flat frequently has to be dressed down with a file when fitting new pins.

These pins go into the crank alternately, that is, if you

look down on the cranks from above the bicycle you should see the nut on one side and the head of the cotterpin on the opposite side.

When removing these pins care has to be taken not to damage the threads—the crank should be supported.

A good tip is for you to use a steel tube long enough to raise one of the wheels off the ground.

The reason for this is that we do not want to risk damaging the bearings in the bracket should the cotter prove stubborn and need some hefty blows to remove it.

When overhauling this kind of bracket hanger, unless so specified it is not necessary to remove the pedals.

Firstly then we drive out the cotters, use a copper mallet or a hammer with a copper block in between.

If the cotters are in good condition and we wish to use them again, a good tip is to put both washers on the right hand cotter so that we know which cotter goes in which crank.

If you have an erecting stand, clamp the bicycle so that you can rest the machine with the left hand side of the bracket uppermost.

Using the "Var" lock ring pliers or a punch, unscrew the lock ring—it has a right hand thread so unscrew to the left—take it off and place it in a container, now unscrew the cup, again it goes to the left.

It will either have 4 holes, in which case, use a peg spanner or wrench—or if it has a raised bar or square section you will recourse to the adjustable wrench—that is, if you do not possess the correct remover.

As you unscrew the cup, place your left hand under the right end of the axle and gently push up; when you feel the cup coming loose, lay down your wrench and continue unscrewing, holding onto the axle as well as the cup.

You will find that you will be able to draw out cup and axle together without losing these balls.

As you do this, put the finger of your left hand up into the right hand cup hole and you will not lose these balls either. Put the cup and axle into your container and slowly withdraw your finger while placing your hand under the cup; now with your right hand finger you can poke inside and push the balls out into the palm of your left hand.

Inspect the right hand cup after cleaning with solvent and a rag—if it is good and installed tightly, there is no reason to disturb it.

If it is pitted or worn proceed to remove following the directions previously described.

Now clean and inspect the axle and left hand cup; if you have to replace these components, there are certain things to take into account.

First and foremost are the threads of the cups.

Probably the most common will be 1-3/8" x 26 T.P.I.; standard Raleigh bracket shells are threaded 1-3/8" x 24 T.P.I.

French brackets are generally threaded 35 x 1, and the Italian are 36 x 24 F.; so check this carefully and do not forget to ascertain whether the right hand cup has a left or right hand thread.

Most cups take 1/4-inch balls, 22 in all (11 on each side); but do not take chances as there are exceptions.

Chater Lea used to make a bracket taking 5/16" balls to name just one.

Next item to check is the axle—overall length, width of the shoulders and length of right hand side—these measurements are all very important and must be scrupulously observed.

To reinstall the bracket set simply reverse the procedure.

Assuming we have either replaced the right hand cup or it is locked tightly in position, smear some grease inside.

Put eleven 1/4-inch balls in the palm of your hand and from underneath push them up into the cup, seat them correctly with the fingers of the other hand, poking down inside the bracket shell.

Now grease the left hand cup and install eleven 1/4-inch

balls and then put the left hand end of the axle through until the shoulder engages them.

Holding the left hand end of the axle, together with the left hand cup, lower it gently into the bracket.

At the same time, the left hand should be underneath the right hand cup, with one finger pushed up through the axle hole; let the axle push your finger out as you begin to screw the cup into shell, in this way no balls will be lost.

Keep a gentle upward pressure on the axle with the left hand until you feel all play removed; now thread on the lock ring.

The right hand chainwheel or wheels and crank goes on next followed by installation of the cotter.

We know which cotter to use, as we took the precaution of putting both washers on the right hand pin.

I like to install the cotter from the top with the crank lying parallel to the chain stay and the bicycle up in the correct position.

This insures that you are pushing against the thick end of the wedge, instead of the thin end and nut.

A general guide for cotter fitting is when the end of the pin is flush with the top of the nut.

With the right hand cotter installed (never tighten the nut to draw the pin through—always give the pin a tap before trying the nut) we can now adjust the axle.

Again it should rotate freely without any play.

Although it is sometimes best to take up the adjustment a trifle on the tight side to allow for setting in, hold the cup with the suitable wrench so that when you tighten the lock ring it does not influence the cup's adjustment.

Finish up with the left hand crank, making sure the cotter goes in the opposite way to the right hand pin.

When both nuts are tightened up check to see whether the cranks line up with each other.

If not, it generally means one of the cotters needs more filing.

EXAMPLE OF COTTERLESS BRACKET SET.

STRONGLIGHT No. 32N – COTTERLESS CRANK AXLE SETS

For 49D & Super Competition 57

NOTE: BALL BEARINGS ARE NOT SHOWN.

Cotterless Crank Axle - - - - -
Right Hand Crank Cup - - - -
Left Hand Crank Cup - - - - -

Left Hand Lock Nut - - - - - - - -
Cotterless Axle Bolt & Washer - - -
Cotterless Crank Dust Cover - - - - -

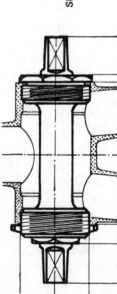

SELECTION OF BOTTOM BRACKET HANGER

When filing cotters take your time and keep the flat on the same plane; it is better to put the pin in and take it out several times, rather than filing too much off at first.

Always check the hole in the crank, it should be a push fit—if the play is too excessive change the crank as this is more prone to wear since it is mild steel as opposed to the axle which is hardened.

Attempts to wrap a piece of shim around the axle to take up play in the crank are not generally successful, since the wear is nearly always uneven to start with.

One thing you can do if the cotters keep indenting is to fit new ones—remove them and then case harden them.

The other bottom-bracket set-up found mostly on higher priced bicycle models but gaining in popularity all the time is the cotterless type.

There have been various methods over the last 20 or 30 years to do away with the time honored method of cotters; triangular ended axles threaded where the crank slides on followed by a nut to name just one.

But the type encountered mostly these days is the square sectioned tapered end favored by such firms as Stronglight, Campagnola, T.A. and a very good copy from Japan (Sugino).

They consist of an axle with shoulders engaging balls in cups similar to the cottered type—the main difference being each end—where the crank is installed.

Now you will see steel cotterless cranks in the same way you can come across aluminum alloy cottered cranks, but in the main cotterless sets use alloy cranks and chainwheels.

Because of this they are more chunky looking, this is to prevent whip and possible breakage if they were made as slender as some of the steel racing cranks.

The crank is fitted with a square cut out section, this fits over the square section of the axle end which has an internal thread and takes a stout hex head bolt, supplied with a washer.

When the bolt is tightened it draws the axle through into the crank—it is important to check this from time to time—it can easily be understood what will happen to the alloy if play is allowed to develop. The outer part of the crank axle aperture is round and threaded, this takes the dust cap and also the tool for removing the crank.

We must make sure we have the right extractors.

Two of the main makes, Stronglight and Campagnolo, both take different tools; however, the Japanese Sugino cotterless set also has the same threads as the Campagnolo so we can use the Italian tool for removing these cranks.

Some removers or remover sets have a two pronged attachment for removing the dust cap—if not, a wide screwdriver can be used.

First of all, we remove this cap which unscrews to the left (The Campagnolo has an Allen socket so use a 5 mm Allen key or wrench to remove this dust cap).

This will expose the hex head of the securing bolt, fit the socket of the remover and unscrew, again to the left.

Remove it completely and be careful not to lose the washer (the Campagnolo bolt is longer than the one used by Stronglight, but if you lose a Stronglight bolt, in an emergency you can use the Campagnolo as a replacement, just remove about 1/4-inch from the end).

Make sure the inner bolt is unscrewed fully from the extractor before threading it into the crank; this goes in right hand.

Now tighten the center bolt, again right hand thread; this will draw the crank off.

This procedure applies to both sides.

For the rest of the overhaul follow the same sequence as for a cottered bracket set.

When replacing the axle in the hanger, be doubly sure you get the chain wheel end in the right side.

Since the cranks are aluminum alloy, make sure they are seated correctly on the axle before fully tightening down the

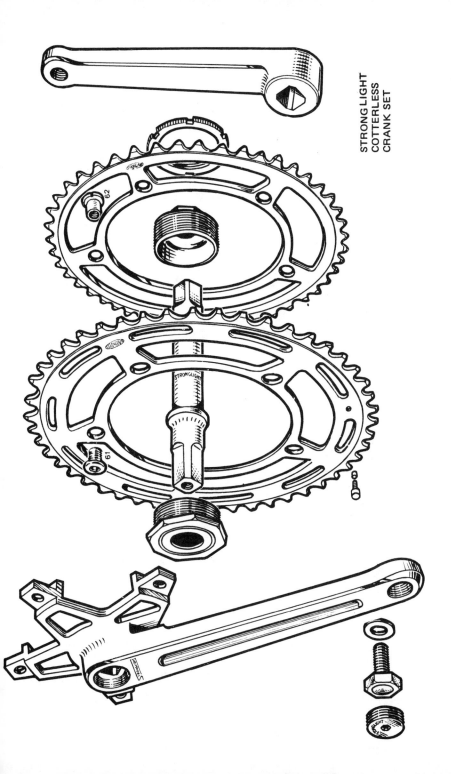

STRONG LIGHT
COTTERLESS
CRANK SET

securing bolt.

When installing new cranks be sure to check these bolts frequently for the first few hundred miles. If they are allowed to work loose the square section can round off, and then you will never be able to keep them tight.

Sometimes we have the case of a good frame perfect in nearly every detail, but with the threads stripped out from the bracket hanger.

What do we do, throw it out? The answer is no!

With a little ingenuity and the right tools we can set the matter straight.

The British company of Baylis Wiley makes a unique bottom-bracket set-up.

This is comprised of a steel-threaded sleeve; the right hand cup which screws into one end of the sleeve differs from the normal cup, inasmuch as it has an inclined shoulder between the flange and the sleeve end.

This is also the case with the lock ring which screws on the left hand cup in the ordinary way.

The only fly in the ointment here is that to install it in our damaged frame we need the right tool to ream out the bracket hanger.

In these days of short supply parts and tools, these reamers might be difficult to come by.

The only suggestion that I can make is for you to use an expanding reamer and adopt a trial and error policy.

When you have reamered the bracket out to the right size, remove the lock ring and slide the unit in and then screw on the lock ring—the two 5-degree tapers on each end bite into the frame and seat it correctly.

As an added security you can drill and tap the bracket shell, preferably from underneath.

Use a 13/64 tap screw in the 1/4" bolt with a lock-washer under the head.

If you cannot obtain the Baylis Wiley bracket axle unit, there is another way that we can get over the difficulty.

Generally it is the left hand thread that strips out, so we find a piece of steel tube just thick enough to take a 5/16-inch universal hex head seat bolt—length should be approximately 1 inch.

In the middle file a concave to correspond to the curvature of the bracket shell with all the insides removed, such as axle cups and balls.

Clean off the paint from the left underside from the shell and with our tube positioned almost flush with the edge of the bracket, that is, at right angles to the axle line.

Bronze weld it and make sure the bronze gets underneath; make a nice fillet all around the tube.

When cool take your hacksaw and make two cuts through the tube and into the bracket shell.

The length should correspond to the depth of the cup when in place and to the final width.

We remove the thin sliver between the cuts which should be approximately 1/16-inch.

To remove the metal between the cuts, drill a hole at the end, and you can even drill this hole before you make your saw cuts.

Just measure the depth of the cup, find the middle of the tube, put your square on the bracket end, scribe a line and center punch and drill using a 3/16-inch drill.

Now set up your bracket in the normal way; through the tube we put our bolt and when tightened this will compensate for the damaged cups and grips the cup.

If anyone thinks this is a Heath Robinson or Rube Goldberg way of doing it, I would remind all and sundry that when I was a boy the new bicycles were still being made with this arrangement on both sides for securing the bottom-bracket assembly.

Concerning the matter of pedal overhaul from the bicycle mechanic's viewpoint, it really is not worth the time to do any major work on them today; unless, they are of the higher priced variety.

To prove our point, it will be noted that most pedals come completely sealed and riveted up—in other words they are not intended to be repaired.

To use a war–time expression, "Just heave 'em away and get a new pair."

The better quality pedals such as Campagnolo and Lyotard are a different proposition; if you can get the spare parts they are well worth overhauling.

Most pedals, speaking mainly of rat-traps or all-metal patterns consist of a frame work roughly oblong in shape through the middle of which passes a barrel generally threaded at one end to receive the dust cap.

I mention metal because they come completely constructed of steel (Chromed) and are entirely of Aluminum Alloy or sometimes A. Alloy frame work and steel barrel.

Before dismantling, it is just as well to check this frame work.

Make sure that the barrel is tight and all the riveted parts are secure—there is no point in overhauling the axle section if the frame part is worn out.

Sometimes when the riveted part is loose it is possible to peen over carefully the heads a little as this will tighten up the frame work, but should the barrel hole be ovaled, there is not much that you can do about it.

Some pedals are purposely made with the plates smooth whereas others have pretty sharpened teeth to grip the shoes.

If you come across the smooth plate pedals, check the make—you may find the pedals old and worn and not worth bothering about.

Satisfying ourselves that the framework is sound (if the corners are bent we can straighten these by merely putting them in the vise and tightening) we can unscrew the dust cap—right hand thread.

These will often times take a wrench, either hex or multi-splined (Campagnolo) or one that is fitted with a screwdriver slot.

On the inside we will find a hex nut, undo this and lift off the washer, next undo the cone.

Generally, I do all this with the flats on the axle in the vise with the pedals held vertically.

In this way, should the nut prove itself stubborn, we can use a little force to unscrew it; this of course applies to the washer and the cone.

When we have removed the cone, hold the top of the axle in one hand and release the vise handle.

We can then lay the pedal on a cloth that we have already spread on the bench.

Gently shake out the balls counting and examining them.

You will by now have realized that the cone end is similar to that of a wheel hub.

Since the lock-washer has the pip on the inside corresponding to the axle groove, the cone is generally more like a miniature one-piece bottom-bracket hanger cone with only a few pedal cones having flats on them.

Most pedals will take 5/32" size balls—but you may come across some older patterns that take 1/8" bearings.

So always check the size and count the number, and also carefully inspect the cups in the hubs.

Finally, check the axle for straightness; the thin end threads for damage; the crank end for possible pits in the fixed cone and naturally, the threads where it screws into the crank.

After carefully cleaning all the bearing surfaces, repack the cups with grease and install the correct number of balls.

If we put in too many bearings the pedal will bind; therefore if in any doubt, fill up the cup until all the balls touch and then remove one.

Insert the axle, placing it back into the vise, either by the flats or by the threads; if by the latter, make sure that we use our vise jaw protectors.

We will assume that we have either obtained new cones or that all of the original parts were in good condition.

PEDALS

CAMPAGNOLO

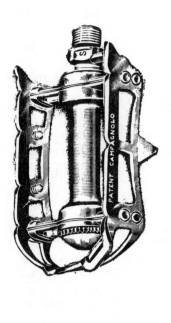

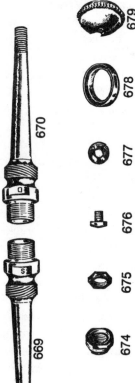

669
670
672
673
674
675

- 669 **Left** hand pedal axle
- 670 **Right** hand pedal axle
- 672 **Inserted** race
- 673 **Pedal** axle washer
- 674 **Pedal** axle cone
- 675 **Pedal** axle lock nut

- 676 **Toe** clip bolt
- 677 **Toe** clip washer
- 678 **Inner** dust cap
- 679 **Pedal** dust cap
- 2103 **Pedal** special ball races

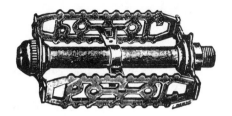

No. 240

TYPICAL
DOUBLE SIDED
RACING PEDAL

No. 23

PLATFORM
PEDAL.

MARCEL   BERTHET

1/8 x ½ Chain,

3/16 x ½ Chain,

HALF LINK

CONNECTING LINK

Next, we replace the cone, screwing it down finger tight following it with the lock-washer and finally the lock-nut.

You will usually find it advantageous to leave the cone slightly loose so that when the nut is tightened this will take up the slack.

Test the pedal by spinning it, if too tight, loosen slightly the lock-nut and with a forked screwdriver back off the cone a little.

Re-tighten the nut and check again, when satisfied, you may replace the dust cups.

Note, that we are speaking of good quality pedals, otherwise, we might have added that on some pedals the dust cap is not threaded but is snapped on and requires being pried off with a screwdriver when we remove it.

By way of interest, rat-trap pedals come in various types, double sided, single sided and "quill". The latter has the side plates curved around into one piece over the dust cap.

And finally the so-called "platform" pedal of which a noted example is the Lyotard "Marcel Berthet."

A further refinement on some pedals is that they are threaded and have two bolts with which to secure toe-clips.

Other pedals merely have holes or spaces for the bolts and washers which are supplied by the toe-clip manufacturers.

Toe-clips are spring-steel clips shaped to fit the toes and balls of the feet and are fastened to the front of the pedal.

These, together with the quick-release straps assist the rider when he is pedalling to keep his feet firmly in place on the pedals.

It is suggested that the rider, if inexperienced, ride his new bicycle until he gets used to it, before installing these aids to pedalling.

He should also learn to disengage his feet quickly when he is coming to a halt.

Toe-clips come generally in 3 lengths or sizes and again the rider should make sure that he gets the right size.

The best way to check for a correct fit is to have the ball of the foot on the pedal when in position.

4

WHEELS, RIMS, SPOKES AND HUBS

Wheels come in all types and sizes. They will vary in size from the small juvenile 16 inch wheel to some models of 12, 14, 16 and 28 inches.

But with few exceptions they are not wheels with adjustable spokes nor are they fitted with pneumatic tires.

The Dunlop Rubber Company at one time listed and made blow-up tires and tubes in these sizes: 12" x 1 3/8", 14"x 1 3/8", 16" x 1 3/8", 18" x 1 3/8", 20" x 1 3/8", 22" x 1 3/8", 24" x 1 3/8", 26" x 1 3/8", 26" x 1 1/4", 26" x 1/2", 26" x 1 3/4", 27" x 1 1/4", and 28" x 1 1/2".

The Dutch manufacture a 12 inch balloon tire for juvenile scooters.

In the main, however, 16 inch wheels are the smallest size that are usually found in the United States.

These are made in lightweight (a term used here to denote anything smaller than middle weight or balloon). In other words, 16" x 1 3/8" and 16" x 1.75" and Schwinn 16" x 1 3/4".

It should be carefully noted when you are buying rubber to get tires that are exactly the same as the old ones. Standard E.A. 3 26" x 1 3/8" tires will not fit on Schwinn 26" x 1 3/8" rims which are in fact E A 1 26" x 1 1/4".

The same applies to all the Schwinn 1 3/4" sizes; 1.75" might mean the same mathematically, but cyclologically, as it were, it does not.

Rims marked S 7 will take only 1 3/4" whereas rims marked S 2 will take both 1.75" or 2.12 5" tires.

Tires that are marked 27" x 1 1/4" will fit any rim that is made for 27 inches, we are of course speaking of rims made for wired-on tires that take seperate inner tubes.

Occasionally, racing type machines will be found with 28 inch rims and tires. These are usually marked 700 C.

Again make sure you purchase 700 C tires and not 27 inch when you need to replace them. This does not apply to the tubes, 27 inch tubes are generally used with 700 C tires.

Most rims are made of steel which is chrome plated. In some cases, especially in cheaper makes, the steel is just painted.

One comes across some Italian junior sizes of rims made of dural, an aluminum alloy, but normally this light metal is restricted to the racing rims such as 27" x 1 1/4", 700 C and a few 26" x 1 3/8".

Besides the lightness of the dural rims, these of course being aluminum will not rust.

Even when left outside to face the elements over a long period of time, and surface erosion happens to set in, it can usually be cleaned and polished by using fine steel wool dipped in metal polish.

Up to now we have touched only on rims and tires of the wired-on variety which are sometimes called "clinchers".

Professional riders and many bike enthusiasts often prefer to use sprint rims fitted with tubular tires, "sprints and tubs". These are more commonly known in America as sew-ups, and in Australia as "singles". They are made in various weights depending on the work for which they are intended.

The chief drawback to this type of tire is that when you get a flat, sew-ups unlike the wired-on tires are not readily repairable on the road.

It is important then for you always to carry spares with you.

In the event of a flat you simply remove the whole tire and replace it with your spare.

Since these sew-up tires are stuck on the rims with cement, it is necessary to make sure the cement is still tacky, otherwise the tire or tires will have to be reglued. (See later chapter on installation of tires).

Still on the subject of rims, years ago, laminated wooden rims were very popular.

If you should ever come across a pair, do not throw them away thinking they are useless—unless of course they are in really bad condition.

Damp weather will severely damage the durability of wooden rims and if you do own a pair remember to guard against this hazard. They should be cleaned off carefully once a year with some very fine sandpaper and then clear lacquered.

If the fancy ever strikes you to replace a bent rim on your bicycle (by this I mean where the rim has reached that stage of not being able to be trued by adjustment of the spokes) always check the number of spokes.

The Junior sizes mostly have 28 spokes per wheel although you will find them with 24 and even 20 spokes.

The majority of wheels that are full-sized take 36 spokes front and rear. But there are bicycles on the market with 32 spokes on the front wheel and 36 or 40 in the rear.

Whenever you go into a bicycle shop for spokes—if only to replace a few broken ones, or your intention is to rebuild the complete wheel—never ask the cycle shop man for a spoke for a wheel of such and such a size.

Different patterns of lacing up wheels are front wheel, direct or radial, crossing, over 2 over 3 over 4; rear wheel generally over 3 or over 4.

It is a good idea either way to take one of the good spokes out and to take it along with you.

If you are going to do a complete rebuilding be sure you also check the pattern.

When you put a new rim on your old hub it is not wise for you to use the old spokes. There are various reasons for this.

If the wheel was built originally with the spokes protruding through the nipples, they would have been ground down flush, leaving a burr on the end of the spokes. When unscrewing the nipple this burr could ruin the thread in the nipple.

You will find also at the head of the spoke where it enters and leaves the hub, that because of stress and strain over a period of time, a groove that is not always visible can accrue.

When rebuilt this can prove to be a weakness as it is now almost certain to be in a different position and angle. Likewise when you replace a spoke always use the new nipple supplied with the spoke since different manufacturers use different threads.

Spokes will come in straight gauge and double-butted and sometimes they are found single-butted.

The idea of double-butted spokes is to give lightness and strength. The spoke is thick at each end and thin in the middle.

Single-butted spokes are usually found on large internal expanding hub brakes, this was very popular with tandems a few years ago.

The thick portion is at the hub end of the spoke to help counteract the heavy stresses when the hub brake is applied.

Regarding the subject of spoking, here too one will find differences of opinions on certain practices.

I specifically refer to lacing. Some people prefer to have their spokes going over and under each other. Others want the spoke to go straight from the hub to the rim.

There are still others who have their spokes tied with fine piano wire where they cross and then soldered. My preference is to have the spoke going straight from hub to rim so that when a shock hits the rim the spokes can glide over each other and give more easily; thus absorbing the impact.

When spokes are laced over and under it will put them in a state of compression.

For the practice of tying and soldering spokes, I can only relate that I have seen wheels that were so constructed, with spoke and nipples torn right through the rim.

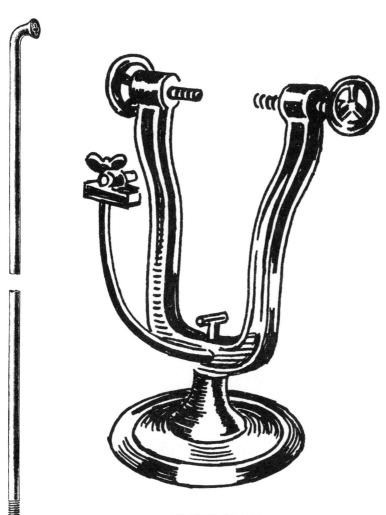

TRUING STAND

Example of a plain gauge spoke

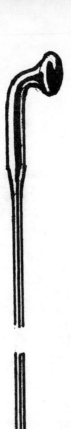

**DOUBLE BUTTED
SPOKE**

**Nipples Only
14 ga. or 15 ga.**

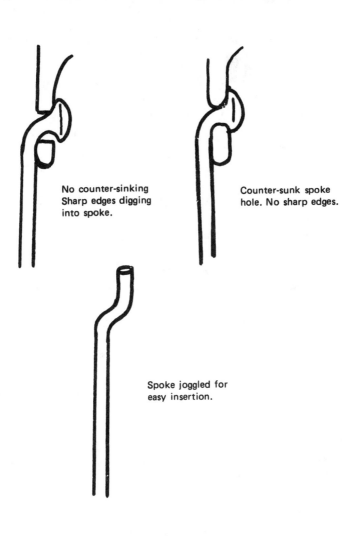

No counter-sinking
Sharp edges digging
into spoke.

Counter-sunk spoke
hole. No sharp edges.

Spoke joggled for
easy insertion.

The only sensible reason for lacing over and under would be on the rear wheel when it is fitted with a multiple freewheel such as a 5-speed cluster; as this will make for a flatter bank of spokes and will assist in the spacing of the gears.

When you find spokes breaking constantly it is usually for two reasons.

First it is because the spokes were made badly to begin with.

When being produced the swaging of the head could have been too severe, this could result in the steel crystallizing. Your remedy here is to replace the lot.

The second reason is that when the hub is made of steel, and in a few instances of hard aluminum alloy, the holes are not counter sunk and the sharp edge is cutting into the spoke.

The remedy is to carefully counter sink the holes on the hub.

As we have just mentioned, hubs are made of steel or alloy. And speaking of front hubs these can be small flanged or large flanged when the bicycle has either hand brakes or rear coaster.

Most lower priced bicycles will have their hubs made of steel whether small or large flanged.

Large flange hubs are supposed to shorten the distance between hub and rim and thus make for a stronger wheel.

You will hear arguments on this for and against.

Riders used to like large flange rear hubs as it made spoke replacement very easy, when they used small or medium cogs the hub flange would show beyond the teeth of the cog.

But today, with so many people using the multiple gears with larger touring cogs of 28 and up, this is no longer possible.

And, too, with so many people using the large disc protectors this prevents the practice of putting in spokes without removing the rear cogs.

REMOVING FREEWHEEL CLUSTERS.

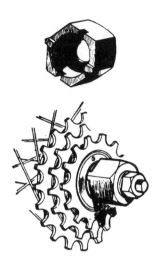

CLUSTER REMOVER

Benelux Freewheel
Remover
Ref. No. F.R.1

CB-1001/FR

INTERNAL SPLINE COG REMOVING TOOLS

Internal Spline, DeLuxe Cog
Removing Tool w/Handle

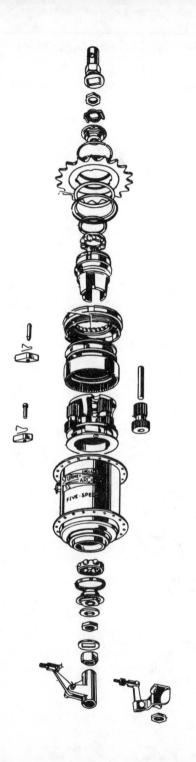

S5 5-SPEED STURMEY-ARCHER HUB

Here a very important factor. If you intend to rebuild your rear wheel and are going to use new spokes in order to do it, remove the rear cluster from the hub before you cut out the old spokes.

You will need a special tool to remove the cogs and in the operation the wheel is used in a leverage capacity.

Once you have cut the spokes out it is very hard indeed to remove the free wheel.

Going back to the front hubs, most will take a 5/16" axle; but these come in a lot of different thread sizes.

Again, be sure to take a sample with you and this will really apply to all bicycle components.

Racing machines of the 10-speed variety take standard European cycle threads front 5/16" x 26 T.P.I. and the rear take 3/8" x 26".

All British bicycles have these thread sizes, with certain exceptions. When the machine is fitted with a front dyno hub or a front brake hub (see subsequent chapter on this type of hub) it will have the rear axle size! The reason for using a heavier axle is simply for strength.

The other reason would be when the rear hub is a Sturmey-Archer 3, 4 or 5-speed. This will take a slightly larger axle that has Raleigh's own special thread.

It is important to know that we have been speaking of axles that are held in the frame and forks with nuts.

Fully equipped racing machines have quick-release axle sets.

I should like to make it clear that when I speak of quick-release, I do not mean wing-nuts.

I am not a lover of wing-nuts. They are not so bad on the front wheel as it is easy for the rider to remove the wheel if he wishes to carry the bicycle in the trunk of his car.

But as for the rear wheel—a definite no. It is very difficult to tighten them up by hand, tight enough so that the wheel will not pull over when the rider is putting his beef into the pedalling.

If you use pliers; what is the sense? Just carry a good wrench and use hex nuts with serrated-washers or track-nuts—these come with the washers attached to the nuts.

As long as we are on the subject of nuts, never put any nut anywhere on a bicycle without first placing a washer underneath.

If you should have trouble with nuts coming loose, try using a spring-washer or a star-washer underneath.

Wing-nuts are not allowed to be used in most races as they can be very dangerous.

I remember seeing a race years ago where several riders collided in a "pile up". One participant had his cheek laid open from another rider's wing-nuts.

Another bad case in point, is the cyclist whose machine is equipped with wing-nuts leaning his bicycle up against another bicycle.

You can imagine the results if the wing nuts catch on the spokes of the machine under it when it is pulled away!

Returning to quick release units, they consist of hollow axles of slightly larger diameter than normal with a double spring-loaded skewer running through, one end of which is a cam operated lever.

The other end is threaded and takes a conical shaped nut to tighten or loosen the throw of the lever.

The axle proper is short enough when on the bicycle to just rest inside the fork ends so that when the lever is snapped tight, only the two inside surfaces of the end pieces are in contact with the out side of the fork ends.

This is very important to remember if you should ever own a bicycle that is equipped with quick-release hubs, and the rear wheel persists in pulling over.

It could be that the axle proper is too long and protrudes slightly through the fork end dropout.

This can be corrected by either carefully cutting off a piece so that the end of the axle is now below the outside of the fork end. A temporary measure, if you do not relish the

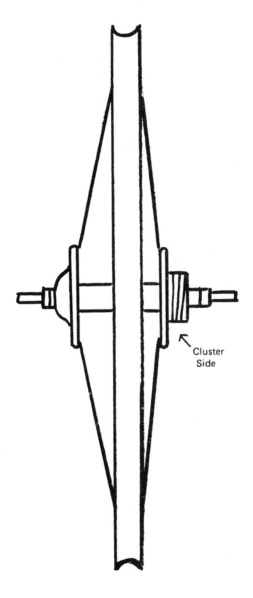

Cluster
Side

Diagram showing rear
wheel with "dish".

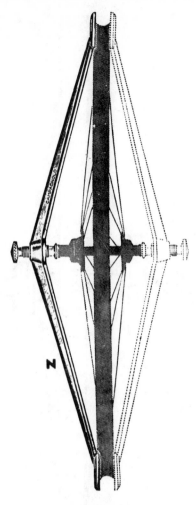

**Wheel Alignment
Tool**

Tool for checking dishing of wheel or centralising rim over
hub, depending on whether rear or front wheel.

idea of cutting the axle, simply remove the lock-nut on the long side, add a washer and then replace the lock-nut.

The only trouble with this method is that it can upset the "dishing" of the wheel, thus causing the wheel to fit off center in the frame.

It should be explained at this point what is meant by "dishing".

In a front wheel the rim is built centrally over the hub making the angle of both sides of the spokes equal.

In other words, assuming the cones have lock-washers and lock-nuts—it does not matter which way you install the wheel—it will run true in the fork.

With a rear wheel, we have to remember that the right side will be fitted with one or more cogs or sprockets up to possibly six.

Therefore this side has to be spaced out accordingly.

In order for the rim to run centrally in the frame it must be moved over to the right until it is central over the two outside cones.

To accomplish this the wheel builder would have tightened the right hand spokes and loosened the left hand spokes.

Thus the angle of the right side should now be shallower than the left side. (See illustration.) The wheel is now dished.

In the past even three-speed hubs had to be dished slightly. Today this is overcome by extending the spacing on the left hand side.

As we have seen, hubs have large and small flanges. We are speaking either of front hubs or rear hubs with just a thread—or in the case of a double sided hub two sets of threads—to which are screwed cogs.

In the case of a track bicycle each side would be double. The main thread which is right hand for the fixed cog and the second thread left hand for the lock-ring.

This will readily be understood as otherwise any backward pressure would unscrew the cog. By having the lock ring screwed on counter clockwise the cog will not unscrew.

On the subject of fixed cogs it is of course assumed that the reader understands what is meant by "fixed". He will understand a cog to be just that, having no mechanism either as part of it or within the hub on which it is threaded.

The rider on the track uses it not only to propel the bicycle in a forward direction but also to control the machine. In a sprint he will balance his cycle while waiting for the "jump" and will also use the cog as a brake.

Track velos are not equipped with normal hand brakes.

On training runs or Time Trial attempts the rider would probably use a roller chain generally 1/2" x 1/8" (modern procedure is going over more to 1/2" x 3/32"). He would use a block chain 1" x 3/16" on the track.

A similar type of hub with only the main thread consisting of a single right hand screw is used on bicycles equipped with derailleur gears.

Years ago double sided hubs—one side for the freewheel and the other for the fixed cog—were very popular. Today in variable geared bicycles the vogue is for single sided hubs. The word "derailleur" is from the French word, which means that the chain literally derails from one cog to another.

The cogs, in this case, two, three, four, five and even six are mounted on a freewheel body which consists of a central boss on the outside, of which is fitted spring loaded pawls.

Since this assembly is mounted inside the ratchet ring, forward drive is gained when the pawls are engaged in the ratchets, and when coasting and freewheeling the pawls lie flat and are disengaged from the ratchets. (See illustration).

I should state here that is possible to find bicycles that are also fitted with single freewheels. These are usually from Great Britain.

In the United States the single freewheel bikes are mostly restricted to junior bicycles and rear chain driven tricycles.

In the types of hubs we have discussed so far, the bearings consist of an axle, 2 cones, ball-bearings, lock-washers and lock-nuts. The last two components keep the cones in correct adjustment.

In the case of the double-sided fixed hub, the distance the cones and locking devices protrude on each side is equal.

But in the derailleur hub, the side the multiple sprockets screw on, the cone and lock-nut has an additional spacer which must extend past the freewheel cluster.

Refer to our discussion on "dishing". The lock-washer consists of either a normal washer with a round hole, jutting out from which is a key that engages in a groove running along the length of the threads on the axle, so that it can slide up and down but can not rotate.

Or the axle is made with flats and the washers have corresponding apertures which again prevent them from turning but not from sliding along.

It should be pointed out here that flats on the axle serve another purpose. They were originally made to fit into fork ends with a 5/16" opening.

With some exceptions most bicycle frame and fork ends are made for 5/16" front and 3/8" rear.

Raleigh until recently made their bicycles to take 5/16" front and rear.

Even their Sturmey-Archer variable speed hubs are built with flat-sided axles measuring 5/16" across the flats.

When these hubs are installed on cycles with 3/8" openings they are fitted with special eared-washers to prevent the axle from turning.

When the bicycle was furnished with a Perry coaster hub which has a 3/8" axle, they solved the problem by putting a canalure on the axle immediately next to the lock-nuts, the depth of which corresponds to the forkend opening.

Going back to the cones and balls, these should be kept in correct adjustment and checked frequently.

The wheel should spin freely without any noticeable side-play at the hub.

A good test is—when lifted from the gound the weight of the valve in the rim should rotate the wheel until it stops with the valve at the 6 o'clock position.

While this works well with the front wheel, sometimes the influence of the chain will negate this test when it is applied to the rear wheel.

Although most cones are adjustable, that is, having flats for use of the cone wrench, it is important wherever possible to keep the right hand cones front and rear securely locked and use only the left hand side for adjustment.

(This also applies to the bottom-bracket hanger cups as we will see when we touch on this part of the bicycle).

Hubs, as with all bearing housings, should be kept packed with good quality medium grade grease.

Depending upon the amount of riding one does, they should be dismantled, cleaned out and repacked at least once a year.

When dismantling, cones and balls should be inspected for wear as a pitted surface will naturally demand a replacement.

The hub cup will generally outlast several cones, nevertheless, cups too should be looked into.

Some cups such as Schwinn front hubs are replaceable, in which case make sure the cup in question is a number 5 or 7.

The damaged cup will have to be forced or knocked out.

To do this, if no. 7, remove dust cap with an old but strong screwdriver.

Try to pry out the old cup. If this fails, make yourself up a punch, (see illustration), and attack it from the inside.

An old axle or gooseneck expander bolt with one side filed away leaving a lip makes a good punch for this operation.

When you replace the new cup, make sure that it fits into the hub straight and true.

A tool can be purchased which consists of a front axle and two pieces of steel, shaped to fit into each cup.

Each piece is drilled to take the axle; a front nut screws on each end of the axle and when tightened pulls the cup or cups into the hub recesses, thus insuring that they are perfectly in alignment with each other.

The number 7 or 5 in common with most United States bearings, comes in a cage so that it is a very simple matter to replace them.

When replacing the ball cages, make sure that you install them correctly with the flat side uppermost; this is identifiable by the manufacturer's printed label.

For the number 5, with the exception of the dust cap which in this case is attached to the cone, follow the same procedure as for the number 7.

Most racing type hubs, however, take loose balls and these are found as follows: 3/16 inch for front hubs with 10 on each side, 1/4 inch for rear hubs with 9 on each side. But here again we have exceptions. Some Austrian-made Steyr bicycles have front hubs which take 7/32" balls and some quick-release hubs take larger balls in front.

Even the same make will on occasion vary. It is always wise that you check and count the balls when dismantling the hub.

Lay the wheel flat, and using a cone wrench, carefully unscrew the left hand lock nut, holding the other side with another cone wrench or crescent wrench on the lock nut.

If you are lucky enough to posess a vise, grip the axle on the right hand side, making sure the jaws are protected with copper or aluminum in order to protect the threads.

Before you remove the axle assembly, I suggest that you spread a cloth on the table or work bench.

This will stop any balls from bouncing that drop out and prevent them from getting lost.

After examining the cones and hub-bearing surfaces, and of course, the balls, make sure that everything is clean.

Should the inside of the hub be hard to get to, wrap a piece of rag around the end of a stick, about the size of the tip of a water-color brush. You will then be able to reach into the recesses.

If your hub has the detachable type dust cap, you will have no problem.

When removing the right hand cone and spacer from the axle, make certain to check the distance at which they are screwed on. But in any case be sure they are locked up tight.

You will now have only the left hand cone to worry about and adjust when reassembling.

Sometimes in order to do this job properly, it may become necessary to remove the freewheel cluster.

Removing the freewheel cluster will also be necessary when you have to replace a broken spoke or spokes on the right hand side; this should be done while the axle is still in the hub.

If you happen to be a bike enthusiast who enjoys doing his own repairs, get yourself a freewheel remover.

As there are so many makes and different types of freewheels on the market, it is important that you buy one that fits perfectly.

For years the clusters had two notches cut out in the center of the boss.

The remover consists of a piece of steel designed to fit over the axle. It has two prongs sticking out that engage the notches. At the other end of the tool are two flats for placing in the vise.

After locking it securely to the freewheel using the axle nut, the wheel is then gripped by the rim at approximately the 9 and 3 o'clock positions, using both hands and then turned counter clockwise.

If the freewheel has been on and not removed for a long period of time, tap the boss all around before you put the remover on. Do this with the wheel supported in the vise and use a blunt punch and hammer.

Many times, a few squirts of penetrating oil—making sure you reach the threaded part—is an excellent idea.

The axle nut should be tightened down securely on the remover until you feel the first movement of the cluster unscrewing.

Now slacken off the nut with each rotation.

When replacing freewheels or cogs, a small amount of grease smeared on threads will help in any future removal.

In the last ten years, more and more freewheels are appearing with the inside of the boss splined.

A bicycle manufacturer in Great Britain seems to have been first to bring out a three-splined freewheel.

Most of the clusters today, however, will be found with multi-splined fittings.

The remover in this case resembles a cog wheel armed with the necessary flats for the vise or wrench. Or for the use of the workshop, it is attached to a long handle that renders powerful leverage.

The only drawback to this otherwise excellent method is that it will generally be necessary to remove the lock-nut and very often the spacer to enable the remover to fit perfectly.

Since the tool fits deeply into the boss, you will not have to use a lock-nut to hold it in place as you remove the cluster. Before leaving this subject, it may be of interest to the reader to mention still another type of hub and freewheel assembly.

I am referring to the freewheel hub wherein the mechanism of the freewheel, consisting of pawls and ratchets, is contained within the hub.

The right hand side is belled out in order to receive the working parts.

The cogs are either offset or screwed on to the protruding shaft with spacers. Or they are splined and held in place with a clip or lock-nut.

This kind of hub has never really become popular. Its excess weight is one of the reasons.

This writer has never come across one that was made of aluminum either here in the United States or in Europe.

The other reason why it has not caught on is because of its bearings.

Hubs of this type have three main bearings.

Besides the two normal outer cone and ball assemblies, the

axle has a double cone and two bearings at the junction of the hub shell along with the clutch mechanism, making it difficult to keep in adjustment.

After removing the freewheel cluster (see notes on removal of freewheels), the first thing to do is check the length of the spokes—take one out and measure it.

You may find with the numerous sizes of hub flanges, shape and thickness of rims, that it is sometimes difficult to get the exact length of spoke.

Bear in mind that the original spokes might have been slightly too long and therefore were ground down.

Most spokes will have the same amount of thread, so if you forgot to check where the end of the spoke came to in the nipple—find a spoke, even if a little longer, than the original, having the same length from head to start of thread.

Remember that its always better to have a spoke slightly longer than shorter in comparison with the old one.

We would like to mention at this point. When building "sew-up" rims, it is very important to be certain that the ends of the spokes are well below the inner surface of the rim.

These rims are constructed differently. Since they are hollow, the two surfaces are connected at spoke holes with bushings, similar in shape and form to hollow rivets.

Another warning that should be remembered. If you experience rims without these bushings, make sure you use the special nipple washers. Otherwise you will find, that the nipples, if used on their own will pull through the rim which in this case is only of single thickness.

Having assured ourselves that we have the right length of spoke, we next check how the wheel was built up to see how many spokes were crossed. (See illustration).

The next step (assuming you are putting a new rim on the wheel) is to count the number of spokes used.

You do not want to get half-way through the job and find that you have either holes to spare or not enough. Also do not guess at the size—It is very easy, if you have 700 C wheels to take it for granted since they are not 26 inch, that they must be 27 inch.

So now we have a hub and a rim with the same number of spoke holes in each, and also a supply of spokes of the correct length.

Looking at the rim you will see that the holes in the rim are staggered, one nearer one side of the rim, the next hole nearer the other.

Remember this as we will be referring to it shortly.

Holding the hub in the left hand (if it has a lubricator, this should be at 6 o'clock) insert a spoke in the hole nearest to the 3 o'clock location, so that the head is uppermost. Take it to the right and nearest of the valve hole and screw on a nipple. Do not tighten nipples all the way down until you have all the spokes installed. (See illustration).

Both rim hole and hub flange should be on the same side.

If the wheel is to be built up over four, we leave six holes on the hub flange.

If, on the other hand, we are crossing three, leave four holes.

Then install the next spoke through the seventh hole (assuming we are building over four). This time do it so that the head is on the inside.

Cross over the first spoke and place the threaded end in the rim. (If you wish to lace, take it underneath the original spoke.) This time leave one hole between both spokes.

Now check to see whether the first spoke is adjacent to the valve hole or is one hole away.

If it is adjacent, the 3rd spoke will go into the vacant hole between the two spokes at the rim.

To ascertain where this 3rd spoke is installed in the hub, hold a seperate spoke across the hub flanges parallel to the hub, and on top of the first spoke you will see that it falls between two holes on the other hub flange.

Put the 3rd spoke in the hub hole to the right of the

seperate spoke; this will then conform to the rim positioning previously mentioned.

If, however, the hole nearest the valve is vacant, you would use the hole to the left of the seperate spoke on the hub.

The fourth spoke goes into the hub, again leaving six holes and crossing the 3rd spoke and is taken to the right of this spoke in the rim.

We now have four spokes going from hub to rim with six holes seperating the spokes on each side of the hub, whereas on the rim they are next to each other.

Starting this way insures that on the completed wheel, the valve hole positioning will be correct.

If the hub has an oiler this will remain upright when the bicycle is hanging up.

Never leave a bicycle standing on its tires; if it is not used for a considerable length of time—hang it up!

This will leave you greater space in the valve hole for finger manipulation of the valve when inflating the tire.

The weight of the valve will swing the wheel (see discussion on hub adjustment) until the valve is at 6 o'clock and then no oil will be able to drip out of the lubricator.

Now put the rest of the inside spokes in on one side of the hub, these will be the ones with heads uppermost.

Starting from the first spoke we installed, leave one hole between each spoke.

Naturally, when we come to the second of the first spokes, we put one on each side.

Next, again using the first spoke as a guide, we put the next spoke closest into the rim being careful to follow the same direction.

Leave three spaces and screw on a nipple, noticing that the rim hole will again be on the side we are using.

I mention spaces and not holes because as we progress the holes will be filled with spokes coming from the opposite side and direction.

When you have all these spokes in their right places, turn

the wheel over and do the same thing again installing the inside spokes first.

You should now have all the "heads" in place with just one "tail" spoke on each side.

The next job is to complete these "tails". Again, do one side at a time.

Place the "tail" spokes in the hub from the inside and again use the first tail spoke as a guide.

Do not forget, if you wish to "lace", place each spoke under the one you cross, and again leave three spaces on the rim.

Another way you can check to see whether you are doing the job in the right sequence is to remember that spokes on the same side, that is, the ones coming from opposite directions do not finish up next to each other on the rim.

When you turn over the rim to put the remaining "tail" spokes in place, you will find, assuming you have all the previous spokes in position correctly, that you merely have to fill up the vacant holes on the rim.

It should be pointed out here that the rim sequence is the same whether you are building over 2, 3 or 4, the only difference being the first positioning of the spokes on the hub.

For the beginner I would suggest starting with a front wheel, or if a rear wheel, a coaster or 3-speed hub.

Rear derailleur wheels with their rather difficult dishing procedure should be left until the novice mechanic has gained some experience.

Correct hub adjustment is important at all times when truing a wheel.

Make sure that you have no side play at the hub, otherwise, this will give you a false reading of the rim where it touches the gauge.

Returning to the completed wheel spoking that we have just finished, the next procedure on the agenda will be to tension up the wheel.

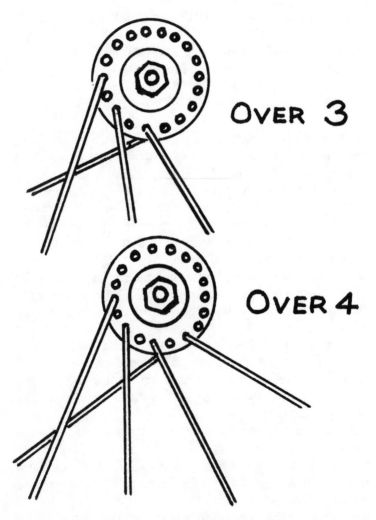

OVER 3

OVER 4

See page 106

Starting at the valve hole, tighten each nipple down to the start of the thread on the spoke.

Never be in a hurry and think that because the spokes feel loose they need a lot of pulling up.

Until you have had some experience, it is much better to go around tightening several times, than to get halfway and then find you have to backtrack and loosen the same spokes.

You might also find a strong temptation to go on tightening.

If this is not checked, permanent warping of the rim (especially if aluminum) is almost a certainty.

Rounding off nipples is another bogey to be guarded against.

Always use a good quality nipple key for excessive tightening, or a spoke wrench—never use pliers.

In some cases where the spokes finish up below the nipple heads, it is good to use a ratchet screwdriver to pull the spokes ready for final tensioning and truing.

After you have gone around tightening all the nipples, the threads on the spokes should no longer be visible. Test the spokes; will they go one or two turns of the wrench?

A good procedure when approaching the valve hole, or have nearly completed the circle, is to observe whether the last few nipples are getting a little harder to tighten.

If this happens, you are now approaching the stage to start truing the wheel.

Should you be fortunate enough to have or know someone with a truing stand—put the wheel in, set the gauge near to the rim and spin the wheel.

As a boy I used an old front fork, pulling open the blades as necessary to accomodate the different hub widths.

I drilled a hole through one blade near the crown and bolted a flat piece of steel about three inches long.

On the other end I tapped a hole to receive a bolt with a wing nut on one end.

This allows both up and down movements and also lateral

adjustment as a rim gauge. (See Illustration).

If the rim hits the gauge, tighten the nearest spoke on the opposite side of the rim.

Should it feel too tight, loosen the spoke on each side nearest the gauge.

Again be careful to do it gradually. Continue to do this until the rim is beginning to spin in a straight manner.

At this point check to see whether the rim is central over the hub.

It is a great bugbear for beginners to keep pulling a rim over until it is dished when it should not be. (See discussion on dishing).

At the same time check to see that you are not developing a "jump" or "hop" in the wheel.

If so, correct this right away by setting the gauge underneath the rim, seeing where it touches and where there is a space.

Starting with the spaces, loosen the spokes at this point in pairs. If after this you still have a place or places where it hits, tighten the spokes again in pairs. But again do this gradually and do not be in a hurry.

If I appear to be repetitive, bear with me for I have found that it is only by repeating pertinent facts that they sink in and register.

When you are satisfied that you have the "jump" removed and that the rim is now central over the hub, return to the lateral truing.

Going back to tightness of spokes, a good test is to pluck them, rather like a harp player.

If the note sounds dull, this means the spoke could do with another ½ or full turn, but check it together with the trueness of the wheel.

Sometimes, due to an imperfect rim it is necessary to leave a spoke or two slightly looser than you would wish.

When you have finished truing the wheel and are satisfied that it is as true as possible, strain it.

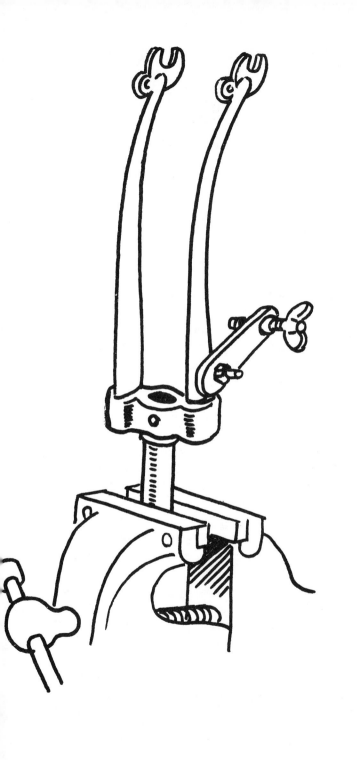

Rest the wheel on some hard object like the floor or bench with the hub and axle upright.

Now rotate the wheel slowly, pressing in a downward direction. When you have gone all around, turn the wheel over and repeat the same procedure.

This is done to seat all the nipples and spoke heads. In fact, you will probably hear a series of pings as they bed down.

Put the wheel back in the stand and again re-true.

In most cases you will find that this is necessary.

If you do this you will find your wheel will stay truer a lot longer.

Otherwise, when riding an unstrained wheel you will find that the shocks sustained from rough roads, pot holes, etc. which you are bound to encounter will unsettle your nicely tuned wheel and put a wobble in it.

The same procedure should be followed, of course, if you are merely truing an old wheel and you should observe the following: If the old rim is "kinked" it is not always possible to true the wheel by spoke manipulation alone.

First, check to see if the rim has any dents or lumps that have been caused by under inflation of the tires and by riding over curbs or depressions in the road.

These can be generally tapped out with a mallet or hammer and a block of wood.

After supporting the rim on the bench, caution is the rule.

Do not just bash at the bump. Use gentle taps, sliding the block of wood under the hammer backwards and forwards to get a nice even surface.

If the rim has a violent bend in it this can be straightened by several methods.

Find the apex of the bend and with this towards you, put your knee on it and with one hand on each side try and straighten the bend.

If the rim is too strong for you to do this, try putting some blocks of wood on the floor so that they support the rim.

HUBS

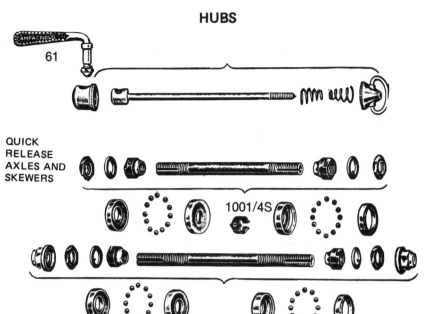

61

QUICK RELEASE AXLES AND SKEWERS

1001/4S

QUICK RELEASE HUB SHOWING HOLLOW AXLE

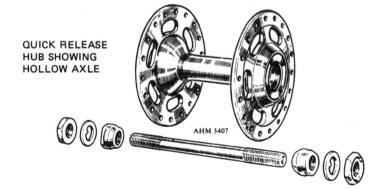

AHM 3407

Place one block on each side of the buckle or bend.

With a friend standing on the wheel rim, put your foot on the bent part and press down.

Sometimes a little persuasion with the mallet or rubber hammer is needed.

Put the wheel back in the truing stand and try truing it with the spokes.

It is often a good idea to loosen the spokes in the bad area before trying to straighten the rim manually.

As in all things experience is the greatest teacher.

A flat spot can sometimes be removed, particularly if the rim is solid. In the case of an aluminum rim, by loosening the spokes in the flat spot area.

Next, get a friend to hold the wheel in a vertical position with the flat spot at 6 o'clock.

Make yourself a block of wood about six inches in length 2 inches wide and approximately 1 inch thick, the end of which has had the corners rounded off.

This should form a curve similar to the inside curvature of the rim.

With the rounded end resting on the rim immediately above the flat spot, give a smart tap on the other end of the wooden mandril.

Once again, use caution—proceed slowly, checking the wheel in the truing stand after each onslaught with the hammer.

When you think you have the rim as good as possible, gradually retighten the spokes, checking for both the lateral and the jump, in the truing stand.

Sometimes when the flat spot is on both sides of the rim, it becomes necessary to remove the spokes completely from the flat spot area so that the block of wood can be placed in the middle of the rim. This will give equal force to each side of the rim when struck.

One final word on the subject of wheel building and truing.

Never forget to check the spoke nipples for possible spoke protrusion before installing rim strip, tire and tube. Even with a strong rim strip, if any of the spokes are sticking through the nipples, eventually they will work their way through the rim strip and pierce the tube.

We have already cautioned you regarding the necessity of correct spoke length when building sew-up rims.

Once a spoke is installed in this type of rim, it is virtually impossible to grind or file it below the surface of the rim if it is too long.

Sometimes the wheel builder finds that no matter how much he tries to true the wheel (and he knows that the rim is in good shape) the wheel just will not true.

A reason might be because of a bent axle. This should always be checked before truing is commenced.

Many times the bend is positioned approximately under one of the cones and is not apparent to the eye. This can only be found by taking this item out of the hub and testing it.

This is accomplished by rolling it slowly on a flat surface.

If you open the top of the vise slightly and rest the axle in the cradle that is formed, you will find it easier to see by slow rotation whether the axle is bent or not.

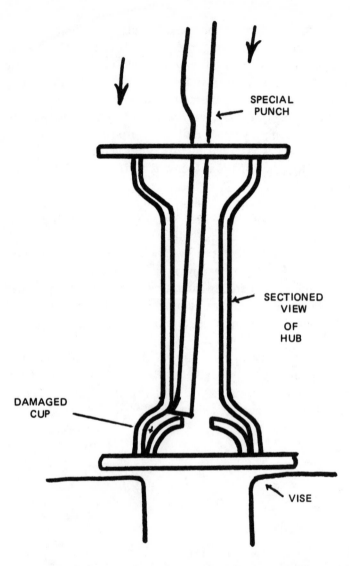

PUNCHING OUT A DAMAGED CUP FROM A HUB

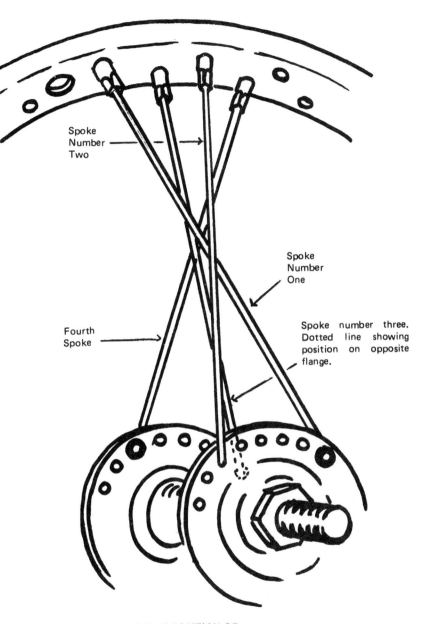

Spoke Number Two

Spoke Number One

Fourth Spoke

Spoke number three. Dotted line showing position on opposite flange.

SHOWING POSITION OF
SPOKES AT VALVE HOLE

5

COASTER HUBS

We have dwelled on front and rear hubs that do not have any inside mechanism, excluding the freewheel hub.

We now turn to the type of hub that also serves to give the rider a method of braking.

We refer, of course, to the coaster-brake or foot-brake hub.

As the cyclist pedals forward in the normal manner, he can if he wishes coast or freewheel. But when he wants to stop, he simply backpedals.

His braking action is caused by means of a clutch inside the hub connected to some kind of brake shoe, disc, et al, which in turn is expanded to either grip the inside of the hub, or grooves or slots which are recessed inside the shell.

There are a great variety of makes and types. As you will discover this pertains to all of the bicycle components.

In the old days most of the hubs had oilers or grease nipples screwed into the middle of the shell.

Nowadays you will find the shells smooth and the hubs packed with grease.

These hubs should be repacked from time to time, depending on the amount of use. Before we examine the different makes in detail we will just run through some simple and minor characteristics.

As we have seen above when dealing with regular hubs, the adjusting side is normally on the left.

In some coaster hubs the adjustment is on the right side and in others it is on the left.

A good rule to go by is as follows: Observe whether the cone on the right is plain or has flats on it. If it has flats it will usually also have a thin lock-nut on the outside. If so, this will be the side by which the bearings are adjusted and this will also be the side on which to dismantle the hub.

Such makes as Bendix, New Departure, Mattatuck, N.K., Shimano are in this category. Other makes such as Perry, Comet and Styria are dismantled from the left hand side.

In order to adjust these, the left hand lock-nut—mostly found in the form of a circular nut with two cut-outs on the side—is loosened and the axle as a whole is rotated either to the left or right.

By gripping the raised square portion at the right end of the axle you can either loosen or tighten the bearings.

To dismantle the hub, unscrew the axle to the left and draw the axle right out after unscrewing the lock-nut and washer completely off the left hand side of the axle.

This washer is mostly keyed, the pip engaging in a groove running the length of the left hand side of the axle. Therefore it can not be rotated but it must be slid along the axle.

The main internals of the above mentioned consist of axle and cone, brake arm side expander, brake cylinder, clutch and driver.

Assuming that you have already done this and now wish to overhaul the hub, the next step is to clean thoroughly all the parts. This includes the ball bearings.

The left hand set is generally in a cage and held in place with a dust cap which can be gently pryed out with a screwdriver. (Perry B100, Schwinn approved MK 1V, and Styria).

On Perry B500, Durex, Komet, and Komet Super, the left-hand ball bearing cage will be found fitted in a canalure on the brake arm expander assembly.

The right-hand ball cage will just simply fall out when the driver is removed.

In a majority of cases, a further set of balls, 10 in number and loose will be seen inside the driver where they are engaged by the right hand cone.

The sprocket in most cases is splined and held on with a

snap ring.

On the older models it is threaded and has a lock-ring in much the same manner as the fixed wheel hub which we described earlier.

When removing sprockets—should it be necessary—always check which side is uppermost.

If flat, check the teeth for chain wear.

If off set, see which side the flange is on. If put back wrongly it could affect the chain line.

After cleaning, including the inside of the hub shell, carefully dry all parts and lay out for inspection. Check all pieces for wear.

The hub of Komet, Super Komet 161 and Schwinn Approved (stamped on the brake arm) should be inspected very carefully for wear and pitting as follows:

Check the inside and bearing surfaces of the hub shell, the brake side expander and stationary cone and driver.

Please note that Komet Super 161 is usually fitted with a ball retainer in the driver.

Check all balls whether they are loose or in cages or in retainers.

A common fault with the brake cylinder is that the ears will break off; these are in the inside and engage the slots in the brake arm expander.

Be sure to check this component for smoothness and weakness of spring, to see whether the axle is bent or has damaged threads.

Inspect the clutch for bad threads, worn serrations, and include the inside threads. Look at the threads on the driver, and check all dust caps for distortion.

See that the brake arm fits snugly on the left hand of the brake arm retarder.

When replacing parts it will be found that we can not always obtain the axle and cone seperately—they mostly come together as a unit.

I must stress here that these two components should be

locked securely to form one piece.

Once having made sure that you have done this, replace all necessary parts and coat the entire assembly well with grease.

Install with loose balls, or in the case of Super 161 a cage, the driver bearing set and tap in dust cap.

Press the ball retainer over the brake arm expander into the canalure.

Do this with slotted end uppermost and the flat side on the ball retainer downwards.

Put on the left hand dust cap followed by the brake arm which should be tapped on in place with a copper mallet.

Next, put the smooth end of the clutch inside the brake cylinder (the opposite end from the ears).

Install these two as a unit into the shell from the left hand side.

Now locate the right hand ball retainer into the hub shell and follow it with the driver; rotate this item to engage in the threads of the clutch.

We can now install the brake arm assembly, making sure the ears of the cylinder engage the slots of the brake arm expander.

While holding the hub together in the left hand, we can now insert the axle through the cog and driver side, rotating it when it hits the left hand expander threads.

Continue screwing until all play is taken up, place keyed washer in place and finally install the lock-nut.

As you hold the squared right hand of the axle in the vise, we can with a "C" or hooked-end wrench tighten up the lock nut, grasping at the same time the brake arm to control adjustment.

Use the same adjustment with all hubs. The wheel should rotate freely without any shake.

If the hub shell was equipped with an oiler and was removed, replace and make sure that the hole is clear.

We will now cover Bendix foot-brake hubs.

Let us assume that the hub we are dismantling is one of

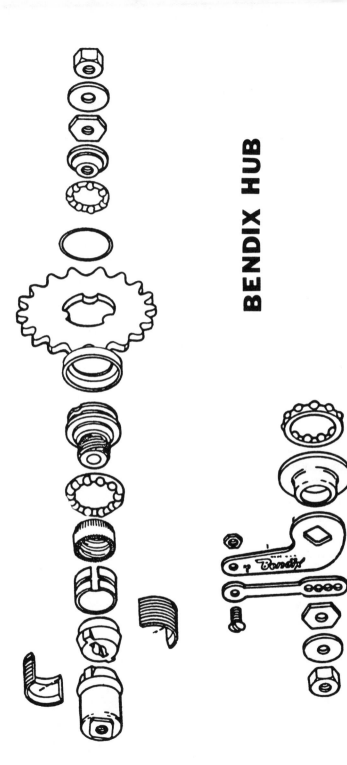

BENDIX HUB

the Bendix single-speed range of hubs.

This would cover the following: Bendix (1946-1961), Bendix RB (1961-1963) and Bendix RB-2 (1963--).

With the outer nuts and washers removed from the axle we hold the hub upright in the vise. Gripping it by the left hand lock-nut (this end has the brake arm), and with the Bendix cone wrench—3/4—we then hold the right hand cone, using the 7/8 cone or adjustable wrench unscrew the right-hand lock-nut. Both of these unscrew counter-clockwise.

Remove both the lock-nut and cone from axle. Rotate driver and cog again counter-clockwise until they disengage.

We can now lift them out of the hub. Lift the small ball retainer from the driver; you will now be able to remove the large bearing ring from the hub.

As we lift the hub shell from the remaining internals, care must be exercised to put our fingers around the now exposed steel brake shoes (two in number).

Lay the wheel with hub shell attached down and remove the brake shoes (Bendix Original and Bendix R.B. Hubs were fitted with brass shoes).

Next, we can remove the clutch assembly from the axle.

If assembly shows signs of damage, dismantle and remove retarder spring from clutch and drive side expander.

On older models, 2 brake shoe keys will be found fitted in slots on the brake arm side expander.

The later practice has been to machine keys on both drive side and brake arm side expanders.

Unless we have to change the axle or the brake arm because of wear, it is generally not necessary to remove these components from each axle.

If we do have to remove them, however, leave the axle in the vise still clamped by the left lock-nut.

Now force the brake arm in counter-clockwise direction. This will break the lock-nut loose.

Remove axle set from vise, turn it over and replace it in the vise; but this time, gripping it in the middle of the axle.

We can now continue removing the lock-nut, following this with the arm, dust cap, ball retainer and brake-arm side expander. Clean thoroughly as we have previously mentioned.

The parts to check for wear and pitting are as follows:

All bearing parts, such as, driver, right-hand cone, brake-arm side expander, hub, shell and ball retainers, should be studied and checked for pitting and wear.

The hub shell should also be checked on the inside for wear and make sure that the hub flanges have not broken loose. (In earlier models the hub shell was in one piece).

Inspect the driver, clutch and drive side expander for chipped or worn threads and worn serrations—especially on these last two items.

Check the axle to see that it is not bent and that the threads are not damaged.

Also inspect for damage the spring that holds the clutch assembly together.

Make sure that the brake shoes are not worn smooth and that they do not have any burrs on the inside tapered surfaces.

Check the brake arm to see that it fits nice and tight on the brake arm expander.

Inspect all dust caps to make sure they are not bent or distorted.

When you are reassembling, replace any parts that show any of the preceding wear marks.

Now grease all parts with a generous coating of a good quality grease.

If the left hand arm assembly was removed, replace it by reversing the dismantling procedure. Leave approximately 1 1/16" of axle protruding from the lock-nut.

Make sure that the manufacturer's name is showing on the outside of the brake arm.

Place the axle assembly upright in the vise, gripping it by the left-hand lock-nut; we can now tighten assembly together by forcing the brake arm in a clockwise direction.

Fit the two halves of the clutch assembly together with retarder spring. And with drive side expander at bottom, install over axle and lower until it touches brake arm expander, making sure the keys line up with each other.

If you are working on an older model, do not forget that the corresponding keys are seperate and fit into slots on the drive side expander and brake arm expander.

Now install the brake shoes so that the inside tapers fit snugly around the top and bottom expanders.

As you hold the shoes in place with one hand, lower the hub shell down and over the assembly until it seats itself correctly over the left hand ball retainer rotating hub shell back and forth to make sure of this.

Next we install the right-hand ball retainer with maker's name uppermost; followed by the driver rotating it to the right to engage the threads on the clutch assembly and to make sure it seats correctly.

We can now insert the small ball retainer, flat part with maker's name uppermost. Follow this with the cone and lock-nut.

With our two Bendix cone wrenches we can adjust and tighten these last two until the wheel rotates freely without any side play. (Note that some mechanics like a trace of side play).

I prefer perfect adjustment, otherwise, the "trace" often develops into a shake after the bicycle has been ridden for a short time.

If the cog was removed, replace after first installing the dust cap.

As we have stated previously, it will either be threaded, multi-splined or three-splined.

The first is held in place with a threaded lock-ring. The second with a "C" spring clip. Lastly and most common today, the cog is held in place with a spring ring.

One final word after overhauling: If the brake works but squeals or squeaks when applied, try some castor oil on the brake shoes.

The Pixie and F & S. Torpedo Boy and Perry 500 Coaster Hubs all work on the same principle as the Komet Hubs.

The main difference is that the right-hand cone is fitted with adjustable slots and is locked in place with a lock-nut of a similar type to the left-hand lock-nut and we need a "C" spanner or wrench to unscrew and tighten it.

It will follow then that there is no squared end on the right-hand end of the axle.

The Pixie and F & S Torpedo Boy which have inter-changeable parts have a keyed washer under the left lock-nut, whereas the Perry 500 does not.

The latter has a different type of driver clutch. It is fitted with an extra retarder spring which is on the outside of the clutch, but when assembled is located inside the brake shoe.

Because of the absence of the squared axle end, we must be very careful when dismantling and assembling to use our copper vise protectors.

Another coaster-brake hub that we sometimes come across is the Centrix.

Once again this design follows very closely the Pixie and Torpedo Boy types of hubs.

The main difference here is in the brake cylinder which is in the form of four curved plates that are held together as a unit by four retarder springs.

The brake arm end has internal ridges which fit into recesses on the brake arm expander.

To remove, pinch the tops of two of the plates together and then press the other two remaining opposite plates towards each other and lift off the brake arm expander. Inspect the cylinder and springs for wear. If we have to replace any of these parts, pointed pliers will come in handy when manipulating the springs.

The Perry B. 100 hub pattern still will be found with numerous manufacturer's names stamped on the brake arm. Once again there is a certain similarity to the Komet design.

The main differences are as follows: Although the axle has the squared end, it has a double thread on the brake arm side.

PERRY B-500 JUVENILE BRAKE

CENTRIX

PERRY B-100 PARTS

The driver has two parts with the outer piece slotted to allow five rollers, which assist the drive, to partially protrude and bear against the inside of the hub shell.

You will also find the cylinder in two parts, although it is sealed together as one unit. The inside part is made of steel and the outer part is made of brass; otherwise, the braking action is the same as it is for the Komet.

Once again we dismantle from the brake arm side by gripping the squared end of the axle in the vise.

Unscrew the lock-nut, lift off the keyed washer and unscrew the brake arm together with the dust cap and brake expander.

It will sometimes be found that the hub is locked and that the brake arm can not be rotated.

In this case we will have to unscrew the right hand cone. And since there are no flats on this item we must utilize the "vise grip".

If we do this with the axle still in the vise, please remember to turn the cone clockwise.

Remove the hub from the vise and with a copper mallet give the axle a good tap. This should drive the hub assembly out of the hub shell as a unit.

As with the previous hubs that we have discussed, you should remove the brake arm from the left-hand cone and dust cap, only if any of these components show signs of wear.

Note that with this type of hub there are two dust caps. You will find one on the brake expander, and one in the hub shell that holds the left-hand ball cage in place.

Do not mistake the canalures on the axle that are immediately adjacent to the left-hand locknut and right-hand cone as worn parts. They have been put there for fitting to frames that have 5/16" rear fork end openings.

Inspect the rest of the components as you would do for the Komet hubs.

If the rollers in the driver or the ball retainer look worn, you remove them by resting the driver on the bench—cog on the bottom—and prying off the spring ring which will now be visible. (If these parts do not show any wear, do not dismantle).

The spring ring is fitted in the circular groove on the driver. You can now carefully lift off the roller cage which will then enable you to take out the five rollers and the ball retainer.

Caution should be used on some of the later Styria hubs as there is no spring circlip or provision for same.

Unless the driver assembly is removed from hub with cog facing downwards, it will fall apart!

If you have to remove dust cap from driver to replace the loose balls, carefully grip the driver in the vise (use your jaw protectors) and with our old standby the screwdriver, pry out the dust cap.

In the older models there was also a grease trap—a felt washer fitted in conjunction with the dust cap.

There should be ten 1/4 inch loose balls. If in any doubt replace all of them.

The cog is held on, in some cases, by the usual spring ring. This can also be pryed off with a screwdriver should it be necessary.

In these older models the driver will be found threaded. To remove them we refer you to our remarks on fixed wheel cogs and lock rings.

Check parts for wear as you would for the Komet hub and inspect all additional components.

Inspect the driver for worn roller cam surfaces and for wear and pitting. If any ball bearings need replacing, replace all five of them.

Inspect the roller cage cam surface for any wear or scars.

Inspect the actuator assembly for scarred or worn cams and check to see that the spring is not damaged.

In order to assemble follow the same directions as for the Komet hubs that we have previously described.

We list here some exceptions and they are as follows:

If the left-hand ball retainer goes into the left-hand side of the hub shell and is held in place with a dust cap, make sure the open side is facing outwards when you are replacing.

The dust cap on the brake arm retarder is installed in the usual way and fits into the hub shell dust cap—this provides a seal.

If the driver assembly was dismantled, proceed as follows:

Grease the driver interior bearing surface and install ten 1/4 inch balls.

Gently tap in dust cap with flat side outwards.

Stand roller cage on bench cams underneath and position five rollers in their slots.

Place ball cage on driver, holding it in place as you lower down driver onto roller cage. Make sure that cams align with rollers.

While you hold assembly together, carefully turn over and with the cog resting on the bench, replace circlip—use a thin screwdriver.

For the remainder of the assembly sequence follow the same directions as you would for the Komet.

Among the numerous coaster brake hubs that a bicycle mechanic will be called upon to service is the retarding type system which uses a disc set. This type of coaster brake hub is still very much in vogue.

The New Departure company was probably the pioneer manufacturer of this system, and advertisements by them dating back to the turn of the century can be found in bicycling magazines of that era.

Although this firm no longer makes hubs, you will find plenty of their products still in use. Other manufacturers who use this system with some minor differences are among the following:

In Japan, they are made by N.K. and Shimano. In the United States they are produced by Mattatuck and Hawthorne.

NEW DEPARTURE TYPE

The main differences are to be found in the ball retainers. If you need to replace these and can not obtain the exact copies, here is a little tip:

If the cages themselves are not completely destroyed, reuse them and replace with new balls. Carefully pinch the tabs of the cage down a little—use a pair of needlenose pliers for this purpose.

The liberal use of grease will also help keep the balls in place until the hub is assembled.

The driver, apart from whether the cog is a splined or threaded fitment, is also slightly different in the Japanese-made hubs.

You will find that the last major difference is the construction of the clutch assembly.

The Mattatuck hub uses a retarder or transfer spring in the shape of a cap for the two units of the clutch to fit into. Most of the others use the traditional clip and tongue type of transfer spring.

This wraps around the bottom half of the clutch (brake clutch), and the projecting tongue fits into a slot on the upper half of the clutch (drive clutch).

Once again, to dismantle, we start from the cog side and you will notice the cone on that side is slotted.

While holding the hub upright in the vise, clamp it by the left-hand lock-nut, unscrew and remove the right-hand lock-nut and cone.

We will need a 5/8" cone wrench and a 7/8" wrench or adjustable type for the lock-nut. (If hub is fitted with the old New Departure lock-nuts we need a 11/16" wrench).

Next, we can remove the driver and cog. Rotate this to the left to disengage the clutch assembly.

If we have to remove the driver ball retainer, a screwdriver is needed to pry off the dust cap.

On the New Departure we remove the threaded lock-nut which also serves as a dust cap. This comes off clockwise and it is best to remove before taking the driver assembly from the hub.

Use a large "C" spanner or blunt drift punch. Remove ball cage from shell and the shell from rest of hub internals.

Lift off clutch assembly followed by the disc set. These discs vary in individual thickness and sometimes number 17 and some hubs will be found with 21 and 28 discs.

The important thing to remember when replacing is that they are in correct sequence, that is, steel, bronze, steel bronze throughout; and that the total thickness is approximately 3/4 inches.

Remove the left-hand ball retainer. And as you do with the other hubs, dismantle left-hand brake arm assembly only if it shows signs of wear.

If you have to remove, follow the same directions for dismantling and reassembling the Bendix.

When you check the parts for wear, you may like to note that I always change the transfer spring and disc set as a matter of course, unless the hub is relatively new.

Inspect all the bearing surfaces such as cones, driver, disc support sleeve and hub shell.

Check all three ball retainers for pitting.

Examine the threads on the driver and clutch assembly, and also the teeth on the latter.

The flats on the disc support sleeve should not be worn—in other words, the discs when mounted must not have too much play.

The dust caps should be checked for distortion.

Examine the brake arm to see that it fits tight and secure on disc support sleeve.

Check the axle—see that it is not bent. Inspect all threaded parts and make sure that they are not stripped or damaged.

Here are some instructions on assembling:

If we dismantled the left-hand arm assembly, we should reassemble the same way as with the Bendix.

Next set the axle with aforementioned component in the vise and grip it by the left-hand lock nut.

Give the brake arm a pull to the right (clockwise). This will make sure brake arm assembly is locked together tight.

Now install ball retainer, flat side downwards on sleeve support cone surface. Follow this with the disc set.

If you are using the old set, check to see that the discs alternate steel, bronze steel, etc.

Now line up all the ears on the discs, and install the clutch assembly with the tapered milled portion uppermost.

Make sure that the tongue of the spring is in the slot, if of that particular pattern.

If it is of the retarder spring cap type, make sure that the flats of cap align with flats on brake clutch.

You will find that there are several methods of replacing the shell over the discs. So try out the different methods and use the one that you find best.

You can use a tool which consists of a tapered threaded sleeve and screws down on the axle and butts up against the discs allowing you to lower the shell down and over with a slight twisting motion.

Now you should find that it seats itself over the left-hand ball retainer. Or you can just simply place the shell down over the axle set and give it a spin.

In most cases you will not have any trouble, but occasionally you may find that the last eared disc will not seat.

If this happens, take the whole assembly out of the vise, and holding it together turn the hub over and waggle the brake arm back and forth—at the same time pressing inwards.

You will know that you have obtained correct seating when the ball retainer can not be seen.

Set the hub back in vise and grip the left-hand lock nut as before.

Now install the right-hand ball retainer with flat side uppermost.

Next we place the driver in position assuming that we have already replaced ball cage and dust cap should it have been necessary to have them removed.

Rotate the drive in a clockwise direction until it seats correctly.

Finally, thread on right-hand cone and lock-nut, holding cone in position while adjusting with cone wrench as you lock the locknut.

When you are working with coaster brakes, always make sure that you use a good serrated washer under the outer hub nuts.

Many manufacturers of low-priced bicycles have used washers of very poor quality. These should be replaced. Make sure the brake arm is securely locked to the chain stay of the bicycle when installing the wheel.

If the brake is squeaky or shudders when applied, and the use of castor oil does not seem to do the trick, I have found that a little graphite worked in and around the discs works very well.

**MAFAC
COMPETITION
BRAKE**

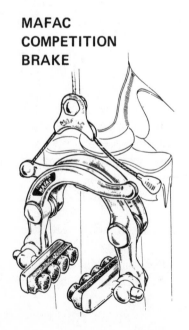

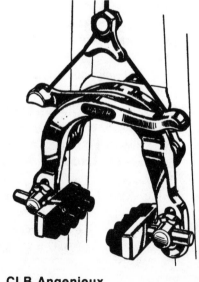

CLB Angenieux

6

HANDBRAKES

Good brakes on a bicycle are of paramount importance as they are on any form of propelled vehicle.

It is the responsibility of the bicycle rider to check or have them checked periodically by a good mechanic.

As we have mentioned previously because of the many component parts that make up the bicycle, there will always be arguments as to the relative merits and faults of each manufacturer's product.

Although there have been quite a number of different ideas on brakes lately—some good, some bad—the two main types that the bicycle mechanic encounters are the side-pull and the center-pull brakes.

The center-pull brake should not be confused with the old Radnall pattern that was found on the low-priced European bicycles several years ago.

We are speaking of the high quality brakes put out by such firms as Mafac, Weinman, Universal and G.B. to name a few.

These manufacturers, in the main, have or still produce brakes in both the center and side-pull systems.

These two systems are the main bone of contention when it comes to deciding which type is best.

Both have their good points and it is just as well to remind those who speak scathingly of side-pulls of the great firm of Campagnola who introduced their newest set of retarders a few years ago. They were side-pull brakes.

Let us examine, first of all, this old stand-by which is also known as "calipers".

The name caliper derives from the engineer's gauge because of its resemblance.

EXAMPLE OF TOURIST SIDE PULL

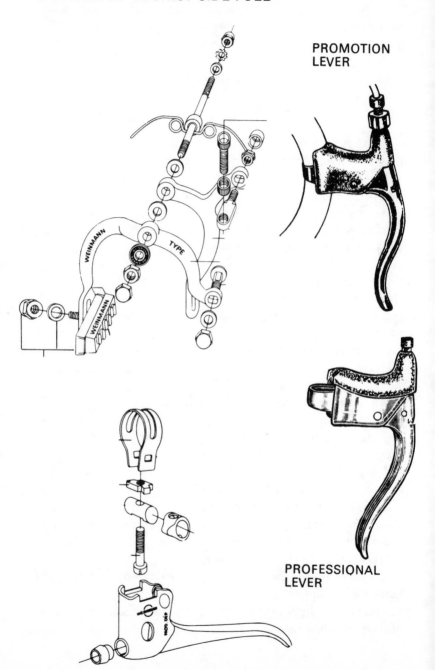

PROMOTION
LEVER

PROFESSIONAL
LEVER

The side-pull brakes have been in existence for many years and have given sterling service.

As in all things there are good and bad side-pull brakes manufactured, and if you are called upon to adjust any of the cheaper types, do not hesitate to inform the customer.

You will find that you can spend a good deal of time, patience and money in trying to get these inferior articles to work properly and still come out with insufficient braking-power.

So do not waste your time and explain to the customer that the only way he will have good brakes is by having new ones installed.

The brakes that I am condemning are those thin steel pieces of rubbish put out on some bicycles from Japan and Italy. They are so weak that you can see the arms bend when you apply them.

Two very good steel side-pull brakes which come to mind are the Raleigh and Phillips. They are a joy to work with.

The calipers and bottom parts follow the same principle as their aluminum alloy counter parts. It is in the levers that the main difference lies.

Until some 35 years ago, most brake levers had the handlebar securing clip sticking out at the side—in some cases both sides.

This was in order to accomodate the securing bolts. Thus the advent of the hooded lever was quite a milestone in bicycle accessories improvement.

In this admirable type of lever, "Lam" (a brake not seen very much in the U.S.A.) was a pioneer. All of the securing bolts, etc., are completely hidden, giving a nice smooth outer surface with no sharp parts to catch on the hand, making it a lot easier to wrap the bars when tape is desired.

When adjusting side-pull brakes, should stiffness be experienced, it is best to disconnect the cable and concentrate on each section.

Start with the calipers. Make sure the center pivot bolt is

not bent or twisted. This will usually be apparent when both block and shoes are parallel to each other but not to the rim when viewed from above.

I should have prefaced these remarks by informing the mechanic to always check the wheels for straightness before adjusting brakes.

If the wheel is out of truth this will give a false reading when adjusting the blocks for closeness to the rim.

Also be sure and check rims for lumps, bumps, dents, etc. (See chapter on wheels).

If the pivot bolt is bent it can generally be straightened, but if too bad it should be replaced, making sure that you obtain the right length and thread.

On the Raleigh type, the bolt goes through the "top hat" sleeve without threading—the only thread is at the rear for the securing nut.

In this case the "top hat" is just long enough to give both arms enough play without being sloppy. If caused by wear there becomes too much play.

Either fit a shim-washer over the "top hat" or reduce its length, but be very careful not to take too much off.

It should be clearly understood that most front and rear brakes are almost similar. The main difference are the length of pivot bolts.

The front bolt has to be long enough to go through the fork crown and have allowances for washers, plain and lock, the tongue of the fender, should fenders or mudguards be fitted. The rear bolt has only to pass through the bridge. Spanning the seat stays; you will come across rear brakes where the securing bolt is seperate from the pivot bolt, the pivot bolt screwing into a block of metal shaped to fit over the bridge.

The securing bolt in this case is vertical; a system, I am afraid, I have no love for.

In the case of the normal horizontal fitting, the bolt sometimes will be found installed with seating pads.

These are thick washers; the inside is concaved to fit the circular bridge. (See section on frames).

With the Phillips type brake, the bolt is threaded along its entire length, thus matching the inside of the "top hat". With the Raleigh you simply make sure that the nut is tight at the rear.

As we have previously stated the length of the "top hat" automatically adjusts the amount of play.

With the Phillips, if the brake is too tight (this is with the cable removed and we are trying the brake calipers with our hand) undo the rear nut and with the right size screwdriver unscrew the bolt a little. On these pattern brakes the head of the bolt is slotted. While keeping the screwdriver in the slot tighten up the rear nut.

Repeat this as is necessary, until the calipers move easily, but without too much play.

Do not forget to oil the pivoting point—put a drop on the spring at each end where it is wrapped around the brake arms.

Now check the brake blocks and shoes.

If single ended the closed end of the shoe must be pointing to the front and the narrow part of the block on top.

In most cases, for example Weinman blocks, the maker's name is embossed on the top side—so the golden rule is printing on the top!

Some firms have been issuing their shoes double ended, or alternately, a seperate piece shaped like an oversize shoe. This fits over the shoe proper; but with its closed end facing the open end of the actual shoe.

The reason for this is as follows: It was found that people like to sit on their bicycles, talking or waiting for the signal, or for traffic to move.

While so engaged they tend to apply their brakes and rock the bicycle back and forth causing the block to sometimes shoot out the open end.

Next check the lever and make sure it is tightly installed on the handlebar.

As previously stated, if the levers are made of steel, the securing screws will be usually visible. Weinman does make a lower priced tourist lever of Aluminum alloy that has the nut and bolt on the side.

You will also find steel hooded levers with internal fastening bolts.

We should always remember that nothing is really "standard" on a bicycle.

The hooded lever type is very simple to tighten. After removing the cable, just pull the lever part towards the handlebars and look inside.

You will find either a slotted bolt head (Weinman or G.B.) or a hex headed bolt or hex nut. The last one is typical of Mafac brakes.

A good workshop should have a Weinman Screwdriver for extra leverage. The manufacturer will even supply a type with a cross handle!

For the other patterns a good selection of spin wrenches (nut drivers) is a must.

Having made sure our lever is firmly secured to the handlebar, in line and level with its corresponding mate, make sure the moveable part is free, but without too much play.

If it is held in place with a nut and bolt this can be used to adjust it.

In most cases the bolt threads into the brake lever housing—the nut serving as a lock nut.

If the lever is too tight, simply back off the locknut and unscrew the bolt slightly—retighten the bolt, check lever and repeat if necessary.

Sometimes tightness can be caused through distortion of the lever where it engages the housing.

If tightness is internal, as in some forms of the hooded lever, this can sometimes be rectified by dismantling the lever from the handlebar.

In many levers the securing bolt passes through the actual

HAND BRAKES

**ADAPTER FOR
VERTICLE HOLE
IN BRIDGE**

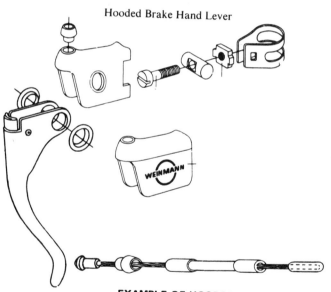

Hooded Brake Hand Lever

WEINMANN

EXAMPLE OF HOODED LEVER

pivot and you can not remove the lever part until this is completely withdrawn. At this point examine the pivot holes.

If lined with nylon washers and they are worn, replace. Straighten this part of the lever if bent, bearing in mind to keep the two holes parallel.

A bar of steel, the correct thickness or width, comes in handy to place between the two arms. Any bends, etc., can be then gently tapped level.

You should know before we leave the lever that when attempting to tighten the lever to the handlebar, and it persists in remaining loose, there are several causes for this, and there are also several remedies.

As we have stated there are two main methods of securing. The C.L.B. (Alp) brakes used to have the lever housing moulded to wrap right around the bar, but I have not seen one of these for some years so I do not think we need to worry about this type of fastening.

The type that has slot headed bolts screws into an eared nut; the two ears in turn fit into a spring band clip. This has a window at each side for the purpose.

Sometimes one of the windows break out in which case the only alternative is to replace the clip.

When you have to do this make sure you obtain the correct size and shape.

Most handlebars come in 7/8" or 15/16" size and occasionally 1" (although there are a few made to accommodate both sizes). Check the number that is usually stamped on the clip; 22 for the 7/8" and 23.5 for the 15/16".

With tourist levers the clamp is normally narrower and sometimes parallel at the point where the windows come.

Sometimes it will be found that by the time you tighten up the bolt the lever becomes stiff and hard to work. You have two alternatives here:

You can take the lever apart and grind off the two ends of the clip, taking care of course to leave enough metal to allow for the strain.

If you do not want to do this or if you do try it and the lever still binds up, cut a section of tin plate to wrap around the bar wide enough for the 4 shoulders of the housing to rest on. In other words, we are increasing the diameter of the handlebars.

If you think this will look unsightly, remember you can cover it up with your handlebar tape.

If, of course, looseness is caused by a broken housing there is not much we can do. We have to replace part or the whole lever.

The other type of lever attachment (Mafac is one) usually has the clip wrapped around the handlebar. The ends, are overlapping, through which passes the bolt. This is attached with a T-section.

One end of the clip is twisted over the T, the other end merely held over the bolt. Apart from when the clip breaks, the only other remedy is to install washers under the nut to give more tightening power on the bolt.

We now come to the cable, which is perhaps, the most important component of the brake.

First of all, let us remember that although most cables today have a nipple at the lever end and an anchor bolt at the caliper end, there was a time when all cables had nipples at each end.

These are still occasionally encountered and it is most likely they will be found on the Raleigh bicycle.

These will have a drum shaped nipple at the lever and a pear shaped nipple at the brake end.

The drawback on this type of arrangement is that it is awkward to lubricate the cable.

Through the years various ideas have been tried; one company even issued their replacement cables fitted with grease nipples.

The only other satisfactory method is to hang the cables up by one end and patiently keep a supply of oil running down inside the casing.

Another disadvantage is the fact that, apart from the adjuster mounted as part and parcel of the cable, we have no other method of shortening or lengthening it.

If the outer casing is too long, we have a bit of a struggle in fitting the cable to the brake.

The best solution is to remove one of the brake blocks. This obviously enables us to compress the calipers and reduce the distance needed when installing the nipples in their sockets.

Incidentally, always make sure that a barrel or drum nipple rotates freely in its socket.

If too tight, dress the outer diameter carefully with a file.

If the nipple is pear-shaped make sure its socket is free.

If the inner wire is too long and we find when adjusting the brake that we are at the end of the adjuster, here are a few tips to give you a little more braking power.

First of all we can replace the cable, provided we have one.

If this is not possible, remove the blocks and shoes and fit another over-washer over the bolt.

But when we replace the blocks and shoes, the additional washer goes under the brake arm, thus making the blocks nearer the rim.

Another remedy, of course, is to unsolder the pear nipple and slide it farther along the inner wire.

To do this we carefully scrape the inner wire, flux it and tin it, and then lay the hot iron on the nipple until the solder starts to melt.

Now, start to push the nipple towards the casing.

Once the solder has melted, the opened strands of the inner wire should stick out from the nipple.

We can now grip these with a pair of pliers and we can use them as a fulcrum against which to lever the nipple along.

Once we have slid the nipple to the required position, we can cut the wire with our side cutters, allowing just enough to stick out; this must be splayed out as was the original end.

Finally drop some fresh solder into this end until it

"blobs" and the nipple resumes its familiar pear shape.

A lot of bother? I agree, but 25 or so years ago, this was common practice and if there is no other way out—at least it is effective.

With the single nipple ended wire, all is plain sailing!

This is the case whether the nipple is drum or pear shaped.

We should make sure that the wire has a thin coating of grease to act as a lubricant.

We must check the outer casing for kinks and whether or not the casing ends are free from "burrs" or "tags" left on by bad cutting.

Naturally, if the inner or outer look at all bad—play it safe and replace them.

You should still check the ends of the casing, and also the inner wire to make sure it is greased.

Now measure the end of the outer casing (even if replacing the old one).

Get a nice curve; do not try, if a rear cable, to follow the contour of the frame too much—avoid abrupt bends.

If too long, examine both ends before shortening, as you may have to trim them both.

Once you have taken a length off from one end, it might make it too short if you trim the other end.

Slip the lever nipple in place. In most cases, you can do this by simply pulling the wire a little way out of the casing and passing it through the lever housing, and then into the nipple socket.

There are some levers that have the nipple socket unslotted, so that you need to have the inner wire completely out of the casing. Pass it up through the bottom of the lever through the socket and out through the cable stop hole in the housing. (Old type C.L.B. and Mafac are two in this category).

If the housing stop is in the form of an adjuster, make sure this is correctly fitted in place and screwed on fully.

Likewise, when the brake lever has rubber hoods make

sure they are fitted correctly.

With the Mafac half-hood, be sure the metal clip is situated in the slot near the handlebar.

Turning to the caliper end of the cable you will find a "3rd hand" (see section on center-pull brakes) comes in handy—if you do not have one—pass the bare end through the adjuster or the upper stop down through the anchor bolt.

Close the caliper with your hand and with your other hand pull the wire through taut. Now gently bend the wire upward and hold it. You can now release the caliper.

This allows you to take your 8 or 9 Weinman wrench and tighten up the anchor bolt.

Now work the lever several times and watch the arms of the caliper—if one block hits the rim before the other there are several remedies to try.

First of all, slacken off the rear securing nut of the pivot bolt and now twist the whole of the brake in the direction that takes the offending block away from the rim. Sometimes it will be found that we have to overdo this.

Now try the brake again. At this point it must be stressed that with some braking systems it is not possible to do this.

I refer to types where the top hat fulcrum and spring holding block are in one, and the face of this is contoured to fit the curvature of the fork crown.

In such cases we can release the end of the spring on the reluctant side and strain it up, then very gently press it back in place.

It is just as well at this point to remember that more and more brakes are being made with a couple of studs for the ends of the spring to rest on, instead of the spring ends being folded to wrap around the brake arms.

For small adjustments it will generally be found that a tap on the shoulders of the spring will suffice to right the offending side.

A notched old screwdriver and hammer will be found handy for this purpose.

Reverting to the cable installation, we should always try when doing this to pull the wire taut enough so that we do not have to make use of the cable adjuster.

Save this for the time when the cable stretches or when the rider is out riding and he does not have a wrench with him.

The adjuster is of course self-explanatory consisting of a threaded barrel, a lock nut and a socket. The latter is sometimes part and parcel of the brake itself.

To tighten the braking action, we simply unscrew the barrel until the correct tension is reached and then lock it in place with the lock nut.

As we have stated, the adjuster can be found on the caliper end or on the brake lever itself.

G.B. brakes have a very good system on their Super Hood levers.

The housing is slotted horizontally enabling a knurled disc to protrude. The adjuster proper is mounted through the middle and is in the usual vertical position.

To adjust we simply turn the disc with our own fingers. The great advantage here is that we can do this even when riding.

Several brakes feature a form of quick-release on some of their models. These in turn are sometimes mounted on the caliper part and sometimes on the levers.

The main idea behind the quick-release is, of course, to enable speedy and easy removal and replacement of wheels.

If the brake blocks are adjusted to the correct distance on each side of the rim, it will be noticed that the tire occupying a larger area than the rim will foul the blocks when the wheel is removed or replaced in the fork.

The quick-release has in the caliper form a lever actuating a cam, the outer edge of which rests under the lip of a smooth barrel with a rear flat surface into which the adjuster is threaded.

When you move the lever up, the narrow part of the cam comes into operation allowing the barrel to descend in its

RALEIGH STEEL BRAKE SHOWING HOOKED TYPE SPRING

IBM NO.	PART NO.	DESCRIPTION	PKG. QTY.
123105	RKD 101	Front Stirrup Assem.	1
123106	RKD 102	Rear Stirrup Assem.	1
123107	RKH 101	R.H. Front Stirrup	6
123108	RKH-102	L.H. Front Stirrup	6
123109	RKH 103	R.H. Rear Stirrup	6
123110	RKH 104	L.H. Rear Stirrup	6
123111	RKM 101	Front Brake Bolt Comp.	6
123112	RKM 102	Rear Brake Bolt Comp.	6
123113	RKM 107	Front Brake Spring	12
123114	RKM 108	Rear Brake Spring	12
123117	RKS 101	Brake Rubber Only	24
156456	RMN 104	Nut For Brake Shoe	36
156457	RMN 108	Plain Brake Bolt Nut	36
123120	RMN 124	Self-Lock Brake Bolt Nut	24
123121	RMW 140	Brake Bushing	12
123122	RMW 142	Rear Packing Washer	12
123123	RMW 144	Front Packing Washer	12
123917	RKP 102	Brake Shoe Comp.	10 prs.
156463	RMW 101	Washer For Brake Bolt	48

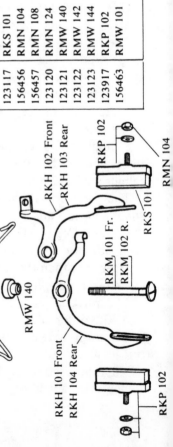

socket.

This lengthens the cable and thus allows the brake to open wider and give greater clearance for the blocks.

When the wheel is replaced (assuming you have removed it for some adjustment or other) you move the lever in the opposite direction.

This brings the large area of the cam into play, raising the barrel, which in turn draws the brake and blocks in closer ready for positive braking.

This form of quick-release was evolved by the Weinman people who later discarded it for their present form which is mounted on the lever.

The Japanese firm Dia Compe now use it on most of their brakes.

The present model of the Weinman Quick-Release works in the following manner:

At the top of the lever itself is a pivoting flange which in the "on" position rests under the lip of the lever housing.

In the "off" position it pivots and slides on inclined ramps and enables the lever to close in closer order, which in turn lengthens the cable and again opens the brake wider.

Let me quote Weinman's own words:

"Your Weinman Quick-Release operates by first squeezing the lever slightly."

"You then push down on the Quick-Release knob and let the lever go into the released position".

"Normal lever position is automatically restored by again squeezing the lever".

Herein lies the beauty of this idea—you can not possibly forget to reinstall your Quick-Release. The moment you use the brake you throw out the Quick-Release.

With the Campagnolo Record side-pull brakes, it could very well be that we have reached the ultimate in braking perfection.

Compact and efficient, they posess several special features which we will mention.

The brake lever clip is somewhat similar to the Mafac type of fitting, with a bolt connected to the clip, and passing through the housing, it is held in place with a hex nut.

The lever pivot is a simple pin in the middle of which is a canalure.

This is for the Keeper Screw (grub screw). This screws immediately below the hex nut that we previously mentioned.

When screwed home the end is accomodated in the canalure of the pivot pin.

The Quick-Release is part and parcel of the anchor bolt assembly, with an eccentric cam after the pattern of the old time Weinman.

But the cable clamp is not of the usual anchor bolt type which consists of a bolt with a hole drilled through it for the wire, and when backed up against the brake arm and tightened down with a nut holding it firm.

In the Campagnolo system we have the Quick-Release unit with a vertical hole for the cable and a horizontal threaded hole butting into it.

This enables the cable clamp bolt to be tightened up against the cable and hold it in the right position.

Projecting from this unit is a threaded pin. This passes through an eccentric sleeve which in turn fits in the orifice at the end of the brake arm.

At the rear of the eccentric sleeve are two flats over which fits the cam lever.

From here it works in much the same manner as the Weinman.

The brake block shoes have an extended piece which provide a guide for quick wheel replacement.

At this point I am sure some reader will turn around and say that I have neglected something.

Up to now we have dealt with the bolt and nut type of pivot bolt.

But of course, the Campagnolo brake along with the G.B.,

Universal, to name just a few, use a different type of pivot.

Instead of screw slotted head the bolt is threaded, on both ends, with the front end taking a flat lock nut followed by a domed nut.

To adjust play the flat nut is tightened or loosened using an open-ended wrench.

Three sizes are common, 10, 11, or 12. Once adjustment is reached, still controlling the nut, tighten the domed nut back on to it.

You will realize here that the pivot bolt is also the fulcrum. The circular block which is slotted to hold the spring is generally integral to the bolt.

Apart from the front adjustment, the rest of the adjustment is the same as we have previously discussed.

Before we leave the side pull-brakes we should mention a minor troublesome detail one often experiences with the front brake.

People can be very careless in the treatment of their bicycles. When they allow their machine to fall heavily to the ground and cause the front wheel to swing around, it can also cause the rear piece of the caliper to hit against the down tube of the frame and bend forward.

When the brake is made of steel it is comparatively easy to straighten. But when made of aluminum alloy, care must be exercised, otherwise it will fracture.

The best way that I have found, after many experiments, is to remove the brake from the fork.

Take off the adjuster and carefully place the arm in the vise with the bent part in the middle and then slowly tighten up the vise so that equal pressure is brought to bear on the whole length.

Another thing to watch is when you replace the spring. If of the curled end variety there is no problem, as you can not put the spring on incorrectly.

But if of the later pattern, such as the type where the ends rest against little stops, make sure the spring is round the right way when you install it in the slot of the fulcrum.

Failure to do this will result in sluggish caliper action.

Do not forget that most manufacturers of brakes issue them in various depths and sizes.

Apart from the lightweight, middleweight and balloon series which are primarily concerned with the tire sizes, the lightweights come in different stirrup depths.

This is because some frame makers leave space for fenders whereas others do not.

And finally, some have exceptionally close tolerances with the tire nearly touching the fork crown.

This means we must be careful to replace broken or weak springs with new ones of the right size and depth.

Do not forget that the rear hole in the seat stay bridge must not be oversized or distorted or the bridge crushed. (See section on frame repairs and brazing in an earlier chapter).

Center-pull brakes, as their name suggests have the pulling power of the cable directed to the center of the brake—the idea being of course to give equal emphasis to each side.

This is accomplished by having two arms of equal length pivoting each side with its own spring.

The arms cross each other and are connected with a small cable, which in turn has a carrier attached to it containing the anchor bolt for the main cable.

Center-pull brakes are relatively trouble free and as long as the pivot bolts are checked and lubricated periodically, they will give efficient service.

Mafac seems to have been the pioneers for the modern center-pull brake and they still possess several noteworthy features.

Whereas most center-pull brakes have their secondary cables of single length with nipples at each end and are non-adjustable, the Mafac has a fixed nipple on one end and is adjustable at its termination. The wire is held by a clamp similar to the main anchor bolt.

The brake blocks and shoes are also adjustable both for

HAND BRAKES

**WEINMANN
CENTER
PULL**

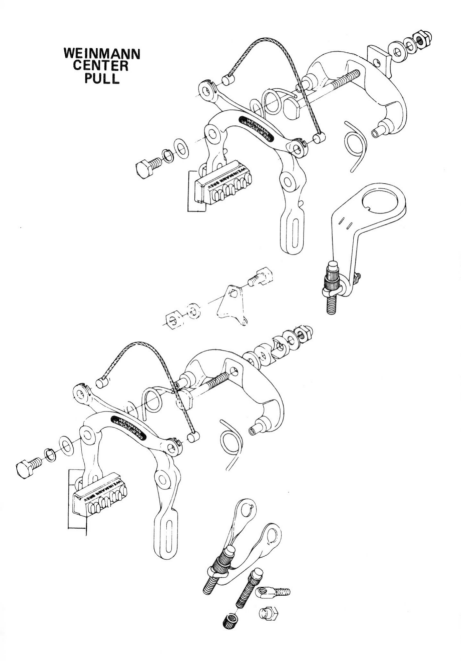

distance to the rim and also for brake depth, they give greater variation should you have a fork or frame with close limits or with more space to fit fenders.

Therefore, it can readily be seen that the Mafac brake with its many features presents an all around serviceable brake and will fit a wide variety of bicycles. If the lever is fitted with a rubber half-hood it will have an extra adjuster.

The Weinman center-pull brake is also excellent, but it must be clearly understood that the right model number must be fitted to match the wheel clearances.

In the category of good center-pull brakes you will also find Universal, Dia Compe and G.B.

One or two points must be observed as we look at the rear brake.

If the cable hanger is not a brazed-on fitment, care must be taken when raising or lowering the seat.

The seat bolt also holds the cable hanger which should be kept parallel to the seat stay.

This should be held when the seat bolt nut is unscrewed and when tightened—otherwise it will influence the cable adjustment.

If the cable wire passes through brazed-on eyes, make sure that they hold the cable casing securely.

Some eyes need to have additional stops to prevent the casing from pulling through.

If at any time an eye breaks off—a temporary repair can be made by using a Sturmey-Archer fulcrum clip and sleeve. Bolt this around the frame tube where the eye has broken off.

Passing on to the front brake, you will find the cable hanger. This fits over the front fork column between the screwed race and locknut.

It sometimes takes the place of the lock ring or washer and has a pip on the inside or a flat to correspond to the groove, or a flat on the column.

This sometimes gets twisted, so carefully straighten it if

this is the case.

Sometimes you will find the extension of the gooseneck drilled and thus acting in place of the hanger.

When adjusting center-pulls "third hand" really comes in handy. This consists of a device which clamps around the brake blocks holding them on to the rim, thus leaving both hands free to adjust the brake.

Observe the same rules for the side pull regarding the lever end. If a quick-release is fitted to the lever, put this out of operation. This will give added purchase when pulling the cable taut.

Assuming that we have installed the cable in the lever and checked the outer casing for correct length and clean ends, pass the inner wire through the outer casing and through any frame eyes, down through the adjuster. If fitted with quick-release on the adjuster, as you did with the lever, throw it out of commission, and into the triangular anchor bolt assembly.

You will find it best to install this component on the secondary wire first and then thread the main wire through.

At this point, check to see that the nipple is still engaged in its socket in the lever.

There is nothing worse than getting the brake end nicely tightened up and then discovering that the nipple has slipped out of the lever.

Pull the wire taut and tighten up the anchor—a word of warning here, get used to the feel of tightening; quite a few aspiring mechanics overtighten and break the bolt!

In many cases the Weinman "8" and "9" wrenches will be found to advantage here.

Sometimes a vise grip suitably adjusted is a good plan for gripping the rear of the bolt while tightening up the front nut.

Remove the third hand and try the brake—do not worry unduly if it feels too tight—I find that a few hefty squeezes on the brake lever will generally loosen it off.

Because of its structure and the rather spongy feel, I find that it is best to have center-pull brake blocks nearer the rim than those of a side-pull.

Here is a tip concerning most cable brakes. If squealing or squeaking is experienced when applying the brakes, get your adjustable wrench, (8" is a nice size,) grip the brake where the blocks fit and gently twist until the front of the block is "toeing in".

Do this to each side—in most cases you will find that this simple adjustment will do the trick.

When removing hooded levers of the Weinman type that have clips with windows—and you do not want to untape and retape the bars—remember that this type of lever is generally installed as a complete unit with just the bolt lose. This can then be slipped over the handlebar and taped when in place.

Again here is where the vise grip comes in handy.

Slip the clip over the handlebar. If taped, gently slide it under the tape at the required position.

Place the eared nut in position and press the open ends together as close as you can with your fingers. While holding it, slip the vise grip over the closed part of the clip until it is about halfway the width of the handlebar. Now clamp it.

Slip the brake lever housing over it and carefully locate the bolt.

You should find that you are now able to screw the bolt into the eared nut quite easily.

Anyone who has tried to do this job without the help of the vise grip will readily appreciate the difference this makes!

Recently there has been a revival of "Safety Levers". These are extensions which fit onto extended lever pivot bolts and enable the bicyclist to use his brakes when riding with his hands on top of dropped handlebars.

It should be stressed that these extensions should be used only in an emergency and not as a normal braking procedure. Because of the distance from the source of the pivoting point to the rider's hand, too much "whip" of the metal will occur.

In other words, do not expect the same braking power, particularly in the rear brake as with the normal lever.

Going back to center-pull adjustments for the moment—if the brake is equipped with safety levers—remove them when making a cable adjustment; this as with the quick-release will facilitate tightening up the anchor bolt.

It should be noted that "Safety Levers" can only be fitted to brake levers of the Weinman and Dia Compe types.

This is because the thick diameter pivot bolt is replaced by an extended pivot of the same thickness.

I have thought of drilling out other levers to the required diameter, but as I have not actually carried out this modification I am reluctant to advise such a step.

The obvious thing to do, should the bicycle come equipped with levers of another design, is to change them to Weinman or Dia-Compe.

Most kits of "Safety Levers" come supplied with new bolts and eared nuts; the reason for this is that a lot of manufacturers thread the bolt on the eared nut, already fitted to the clip and then swage over the end of the bolt to prevent losing the nut.

It will readily be understood what will happen should this bolt and nut be used again.

When fitting this component be sure to follow the directions that come with the kit.

However, it will be found sometimes that it is necessary to bend the end of the "Safety Lever" where it fits under the lip of the main lever.

Always make sure the little coiled spring is fitted inside the open end of the pivot pin; this acts rather in the manner of a locking device for the Phillips head securing bolt.

It will be found that by changing the position of the main lever you can regulate the distance of the "Safety Lever" to the handlebar.

This will be found to be a distinct advantage, especially for people who have a small reach.

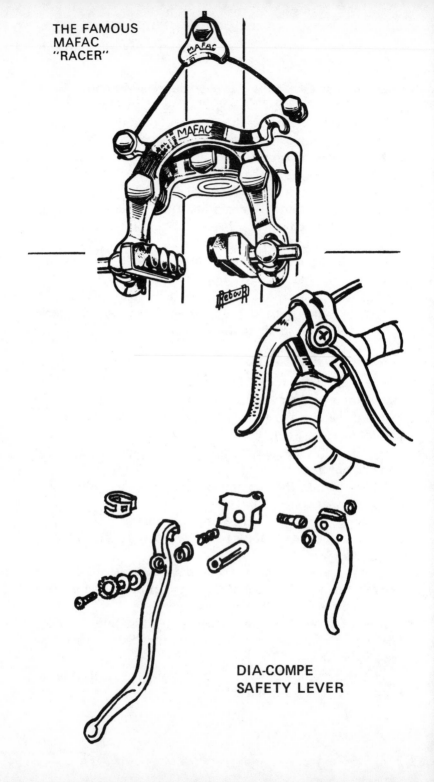

THE FAMOUS
MAFAC
"RACER"

DIA-COMPE
SAFETY LEVER

7

DERAILLEURS AND GEARS

Bicycling has been described as "geared walking" and if you just need the bicycle for short trips to the store, etc., a single-speed machine is fine. But for rides of longer distances and especially when the terain is undulating, you really need a variable geared bicycle. There are three-speed, four-speed and even five-speed hubs of the epicyclic principle.

These are very helpful and useful.

But for really long rides, for all types of road racing or touring where one experiences complete changes of topography an "open gear" or derailleur principle is best.

Some reasons are as follows: With a hub gear the ratios are fixed so that even if you change the cog you only make all the gears higher or lower depending on the size of cog you install.

With a derailleur however, you can specify (when supplies are normal) how many teeth you want—if practical—on each cog thus making the ratios fit your particular needs.

Generally speaking, it is lighter than the hub gear and easier to see what is wrong if the gears slip or do not change.

With a hub gear, if you have tried the correct cable adjustment and it still slips or malfunctions in any way—the hub will have to be dismantled.

This is not an easy task when you do not have the "know-how" to carry out this procedure.

There are disadvantages to be considered with the open gear that one encounters.

The open gear is susceptable to damage when the bicycle falls over on its right side.

Always check the gear when this happens.

Since the gear is open and exposed to the elements it collects dirt and rust when the machine is ridden in rainy weather.

At such times you should keep a slightly oily rag handy to give the gear a good wiping over.

Please note the word derailleur constitutes a type and not make of gear.

People are constantly going into bicycle shops asking for a derailleur cable and when they are asked the make, they name the make of the bicycle.

There have been bicycle manufacturers in the past who made their own gears.

Two come to mind. Hercules, with their Hercumatic, and B.S.A. (no connection with the B.S.A. 3-speed hub)! But in the main most bicycle makers fit a seperate recognized make of gear.

When you need a cable or gear wire or any spare part for your gear, either take the broken part with you or quote the make and model of the derailleur which is nearly always found stamped or embossed on the gear system.

A word of caution regarding gear wires: If you bought your machine used, remember that the gear system could have been replaced with a different make or type.

For example, suppose the machine was originally equipped with Simplex gears and for some reason the rider replaced the bottom part with a Huret Allvit.

As the new owner of this machine you will find that if you need a new wire the modern Simplex gear levers will take a different shaped nipple than the Huret Allvit kind.

So be sure that you check your levers.

As we have explained earlier (See seperate section on hubs), the word derailleur is derived from the French, meaning to derail from one cog to another.

There are several different makes on the market and invariably the question arises as to which one is the best!

Wherever cyclists get together, or for that matter even

bicycle mechanics, one is sure to hear different opinions.

Some will swear by one make and others by another make.

But whatever the make, certain rules must be followed to see that the gears work correctly.

The idea of fitting the rear hub with a number of sprockets, causing the chain to jump from one to another seems to have been first thought of in the 1880's by an Englishman named George Davies.

But as Paul de Vivie of France perfected it, most people associate the derailleur with that country and use the French designation.

But basically the gear consists of a given number of cogs on the rear hub together with a moveable spring loaded cage which in turn houses two rollers.

At least most gears, these days, use two rollers. (The Cyclo-Olympic and Campagnolo Sport had just the one roller).

There are two reasons for the spring loading type.

The first is for tensioning the chain when it is being switched by means of the cable operated cage from one cog of 14 teeth to another of 25 teeth and eventually to one of 30 teeth. The second is to return the gear to its original position.

We have spoken of the cogs on the rear which can vary in number, but presently the five-gear cluster is very popular.

A foreign firm (Bianchi of Italy) has produced a great many machines with 6 cog clusters.

We must not forget the front chain wheel or sprocket.

If it is single with a five on the rear, it is naturally a five-speed.

If we have two on the front with the same combination on the rear it becomes a 10-speed, and with 3 on the front you would have a 15-speed.

When the chain is on the largest of the front chainwheels and on the smallest of the rear cogs you are in top or high gear—this means the pedalling is hard and should be only used on flat or down grades.—If the wind is behind you, a faster speed, of course, will be attained.

However, if the chain is on the smallest of the front sprockets (chainwheel) and on the largest rear cog you will be in low or bottom gear.

Here the pedalling is easy and should only be used when the going is very hard—such as going up a steep hill or when facing an oncoming wind.

These are the two extremes in gear usage.

The intermediate gears should be used accordingly.

Without straining yourself, it is good policy to use as high a gear as is possible. In other words, do not drop down to bottom gear as soon as the going gets tough—as it could easily become even tougher and then you would have no lower gears in reserve.

Gears are calculated by dividing the number of teeth on the front sprocket by the number of teeth on the rear cog and then multiplying that number by the diameter of the rear wheel.

Should you wish to go further into the subject and would like to know the actual distance travelled in inches, this is how to do it!

Every time you make a complete pedal revolution, just multiply gear derived at by the above calculation by Pi (3.1 1/7.) For quick reference we are providing a gear table for the reader's convenience.

While each make of derailleur possesses some characteristics of its own, today all the rear gears work on the parallelogram principle.

This was not always so. Some years ago a firm calling its product "Triavellox" developed a rear gear wherein the spring tensioning device remained stationary when the gears where changed.

The sprockets themselves sliding from side to side on a splined shaft were actuated by a little spring loaded chain and rod contained in the hollow axle, rather like the style of the

CAMPAGNOLO
FRONT CHANGERS

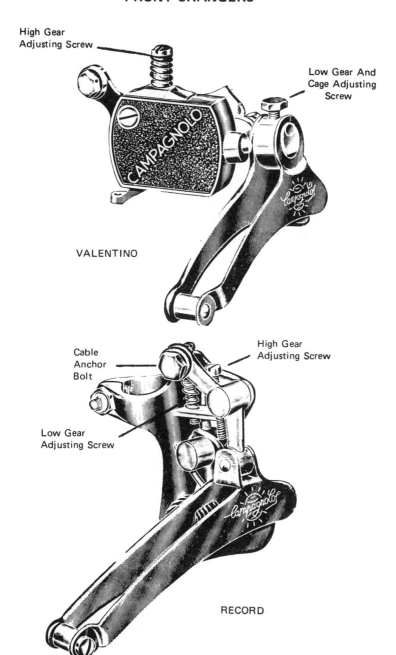

High Gear
Adjusting Screw

Low Gear And
Cage Adjusting
Screw

VALENTINO

Cable
Anchor
Bolt

High Gear
Adjusting Screw

Low Gear
Adjusting Screw

RECORD

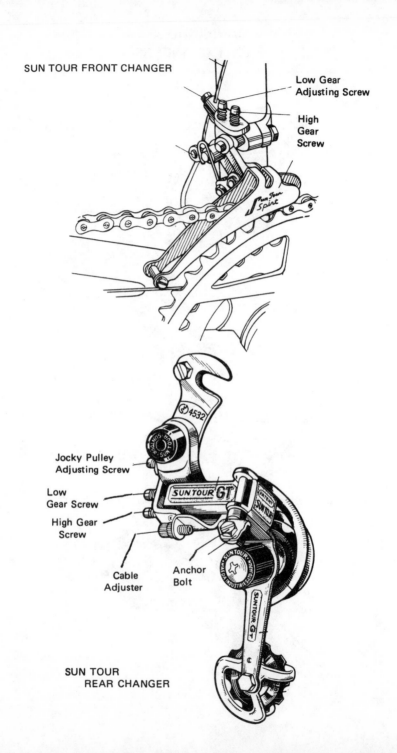

SUN TOUR FRONT CHANGER

Low Gear
Adjusting Screw

High
Gear
Screw

Jocky Pulley
Adjusting Screw

Low
Gear Screw

High Gear
Screw

Cable
Adjuster

Anchor
Bolt

SUN TOUR
REAR CHANGER

Sturmey-Archer A.W. 3-speed control.

Weight seems to have ruled against this system ever becoming popular.

It did, however, have one important factor that no other derailleur has; with each gear change the front chain wheel and rear cog selected were in perfect alignment.

Another type that comes to mind is the Osgear, named after the Frenchman Oscar Egg.

In this arrangement, the rear hub is fitted with the normal freewheel cluster; but the chain tensioning device is in the form of a spring loaded arm positioned under the bottom-bracket hanger and on the inside of the front chain wheel.

The gear changer proper is in the form of a swivelling two-pronged fork mounted on the underside of the chain stay.

The chain passes through the fork prongs which when swivelled by means of a cable and lever, shift the chain from one rear sprocket to the next.

There was even a special pattern rear fork end to be used in conjunction with this gear.

These can readily be recognized by the two spurs sticking down directly in front of the dropout slot.

With wheel removal the wheel dropped down and out and could not go forward into the gear changer.

Other systems have also been tried.

The majority of derailleurs in use before the parallelogram principle came into vogue used the coiled spring wrapped around the actuating shaft idea.

The spring generally fullfilled two functions; chain tensioning and recuperating the gear cage.

The actuating shaft and spring were contained within an adjustable barrel and it was herein that the weakness lay.

Wear developed very quickly between the shaft and barrel causing sloppiness which in turn caused bad alignment.

The spring if left in a compressed state (in this form of gear with the lever forward the chain is on the large rear cog)

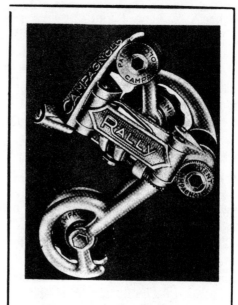

CAMPAGNOLO RALLY DERAILLEUR

REAR TEETH CAPACITY
13-36

FRONT CAPACITY
36-54

CAMPAGNOLO
REAR DERAILEURS

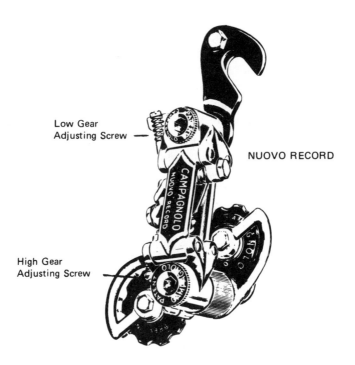

Low Gear
Adjusting Screw —

NUOVO RECORD

High Gear
Adjusting Screw

SUPER RECORD

became distorted and weak and would not return the cage to the large cog or low gear.

When I think of the old days and the headaches in trying to repair and adjust this form of gear system and contrast it to the excellent form now in use, I can only wish that they had invented the parallelogram a lot earlier.

If your gear does not perform correctly, several points should be checked. Alignment is the most important factor.

First and foremost, the middle of the freewheel cluster should be dead-in-line with the middle of the front sprocket or sprockets.

If it is a 5-speed, the middle cog should line up perfectly with the front sprocket.

If a 10-speed, a line should be drawn between the front two chain wheels.

And if a 15-speed, the middle cogs—front and rear—should be perfectly in line.

This can be done by getting down behind the rear cluster and sighting through to the front sprocket by eye.

When this is not so, it is advisable to first check the bicycle frame for perfect tracking (See notes on frames).

If the frame is found to be in track, the next thing to do is check the spacing on the rear cluster.

Can this be changed? This will depend on whether the freewheel needs to be moved nearer to the center of the wheel or pulled out farther.

Several things have to be taken into consideration here.

The thread of the hub to which the cluster screws on to has only a certain number of threads.

Therefore, when we wish to move the freewheel out we must remember that you do not want this important unit to be dependent on just a couple of threads, especially when the hub is made of aluminum alloy.

In view of this contingency use spacing washers behind the cluster with care.

Another point also comes to mind here.

If you are using one of those large chrome spoke protectors, remember that some of them (the disc made by Schwinn is a case in point) have a raised portion where it fits over the hub corresponding with the shoulder marking the end of the threaded part of the hub. This in itself can be a spacer.

When fitting discs of these types check to see that the depth of the shoulder is the same as the raised portion of the disc.

When the hub shoulder is shallower be sure to fit the spring that is supplied with the protector; this butts up against the shoulder and increases the depth or thickness of it.

Failure to install this ring on a hub with shallow shoulders will result in squashing the center of the protector and will cause the rest to bow outwards, necessitating in unnecessary spacing to prevent the disc from fouling the gear cage when in low gear.

We now consider the question of spacing on the hub axle. We are now, of course, looking at the high gear end of the cluster.

Here again several things have to be thought of. Length of axle is one thing.

If we wish to increase the spacing, we must ask ourselves— is the axle long enough?

We must have enough room for a serrated-washer and nut after allowing for the thickness of the dropout and gear plate.

Or, alternately, we must have enough stub axle sticking out should we be using a quck-release set-up.

When decreasing packing or spacers on the axle, care should be exercised.

Otherwise, on some rear ends with close tolerances there could be fouling with the small cog.

Fender brace bolts, when used particularly in conjunction with carrier racks should also be checked.

At the risk of looking unsightly, it is a good plan with the latter to use bolts with flat heads and insert them from the inside, and installing any nuts, washers, etc. on the outside.

Reverting to the rear axle—it will be noticed that I have not mentioned wing-nuts. In an earlier chapter I gave my reasons for not using wing-nuts on the rear of a bicycle.

In addition, let me say here—unless they are of a special pattern and made especially for the purpose—it will be found that difficulty can be experienced in tightening these fittings up; particularly on the right side when the wings will catch against the gear system.

Returning to the alignment of cogs and sprockets, in some cases it is possible to alter the position of front chainwheel or chainwheels.

With the cottered variety a certain leeway will be found with most axles—the cotter pin slot being wide enough to enable the crank to be moved in or out a little.

This is done by removing the cotter pin, sliding the crank to the position you want and then trying to replace the cotter.

If this is not practical, another alternative is to replace the Bottom-Bracket axle, making sure that the shoulders are the same distance apart.

Some well known makes of Bottom-Bracket hanger axles supply several chain line lengths making it relatively simple. Again care must be taken in not trying to install too short an axle, especially, if the chain stay is not indented. Otherwise, the teeth part of the sprocket will rub on the stay.

This applies, of course, to cotterless sets where the chainwheel and crank have to be tightened down onto the axle and set in the one position.

If the stay is not indented and the chainwheel rubs only slightly, it is possible to make an indentation.

In order to do this, find an old cold chisel and using the circular grinder remove the sharp edge.

Now make a nice rounded tip. This can be accomplished by holding the chisel at right angles to the grindstone and carefully moving the other end up and down.

Make a mark with chalk on the stay, the position and length that you want the slot to be. While carefully holding the chisel on the stay with the flat part horizontal, give a smart but controlled tap with a hammer.

Depending on how wide your chisel is and how long you want the indentation, keep tapping with the hammer until the flute is of the required length and depth.

Speaking of spacing—this can sometimes be a problem, regarding the distance between the front sprockets.

This will be found sometimes to be excessive, causing the chain to drop down between the two cogs.

This can be rectified by using several methods.

First check the inside small cog.

In most cases it will be flat one side and shouldered and offset on the other.

If the flat part is on the side nearest the bicycle you can reduce the spacing by undoing the bolts and simply reversing it.

The offset shouldered side will now be facing inward.

If this is not possible, again remove the bolts and reduce the thickness of the spaces, usually small sleeves made of alloy. Be careful not to make them too small and also to keep them uniform.

Otherwise, in the first instance, chain rubbing will result. In the second, the two rings will not be parallel.

One further method is teeth manipulation.

Among your tools should be a tooth stick—this is something you should be able to make yourself.

A piece of steel rod approximately 5/16 inches thick and roughly a foot long is secured.

Now carefully cut a slot in one end.

This should be about 3/4 inches in depth and just wide enough to go over one of the teeth.

At this point it should be noted that most derailleur gears today use 3/32 inch chains.

This is the narrow width as opposed to 1/8 inch gauge used on single-speed and variable speed hubs.

It is, however, possible to find older 3 and 4-speeds using the wider chain.

One Japanese firm has issued gear set-ups for 5-speeds using a cluster with the first two small cogs 1/8 inch, the remaining 3 for 3/32" chain, but the chain used is 1/8 inch.

Sometimes these clusters are sent seperately but are included in the order for 3/32" freewheels.

It will be readily understood the mixup that will result should the mechanic not notice the difference and tries to install one of these beauties on a normal 10-speed set-up.

But let us now return to our tooth stick tool.

Once we have made sure that the slot is just right and fits over the teeth, we can then bend the slotted end to an angle of about 30 degrees.

This will give more room for manipulation.

If the chain drops between the two front cogs only occasionally—or the spacing is only very slightly out—or even if only one or two teeth are out chain jumps will occur.

This last fault can also apply to the rear cluster.

Now by using our tooth stick we can gently bend, straighten or rectify all or any defective teeth on the inside or outside of the front sprockets, or as we have said the rear cluster also.

By gently setting the teeth on the inside front cog towards the outer ring we can decrease the spacing.

Attention should always be paid to the bolts that secure the front sprocket or sprockets to the crank.

These are sometimes the same bolts that also hold the two rings together.

Please note that in some cases there are two sets of bolts, washers and nuts. Some will also be found with the two rings riveted together.

But whatever method is used, so long as these are nuts and bolts, these should be carefully checked and tightened up accordingly.

On some of the lower priced sets, a good plan after tightening, will be to rest the head of the bolt on some hard object and center-punch the middle of the other end.

Nothing is worse than the bicycle rider suddenly finding that his sprockets are coming loose and possibly losing one or more of the bolts. This can prove to be a disaster, especially when spare parts are in short supply.

Once we have established that the bolts on the chainwheels are fully tightened and the spacers are correctly positioned, we should check to see that the chainwheel or wheels—depending on how many gears we have—are true and will spin straight.

If they are out of truth, this could be the cause for chain derailment such as the dropping off of the smaller front ring on to the inside or similarly causing the chain to fall off the large outer ring.

Unless chainwheels are very badly distorted they usually can be straightened.

It will very often be found that the main point of distortion occurs at one of the three pin or bolt attachments.

By spinning the chainwheel we can determine which way the ring is out. Using good judgement and a block of wood and hammer we can rectify the buckle.

Sometimes the two rings will not be parallel—here you will go for the outer ring first—using the cage of the front changer as a guide.

Rubber and copper mallets will also be very useful in this line of work.

After truing the outer ring to our satisfaction, we next check the inner ring.

Portions of this ring between the bolts are normally the chief offenders.

A screwdriver carefully placed between the rings can be used to pry out the faulty part.

Let us add that it is not uncommon for new front

sprockets to need straightening and this is especially true among the lower priced sets.

Returning once again to the chain, it must be understood that all derailleur chains must be endless and that the join should be riveted. And one should never use a normal spring or master link.

When rivetting up a chain, always test the join afterwards to make sure that it is perfectly free and flexible. If tight, hold each side of the riveted part in each hand and strain the chain sideways. Do this with the join in various positions; thus insuring that the chain will curve in and out and around all the cogs and pulley wheels in the rear cage.

Always check to see that the chain is not twisted. Sometimes this can be rectified by holding the chain at the comencement of the twist with a "vise-grip", having each end of the rivet between the jaws.

Do likewise to the other end of the offending portion. (In other words, we are using two "vise-grips".)

You should now be able to gently straighten out the chain.

But if the chain is old, don't waste time: Replace it!

This brings up the old adage.

"If you change the chain you should change the rear cogs."

Otherwise, "slipping" or chain "jumping" will result, particularly in the smaller ratios.

At best you will be lucky if the transmission does not grind.

Returning once again to the chain, it must be understood that all derailleur chains must be endless and that the join should be riveted.

And one should never use a normal spring or master link. When riveting up a chain, always test the join afterwards to make sure that it is perfectly free and flexible.

If tight, hold each side of the riveted part in each hand and strain the chain sideways.

Do this with the join in various positions, thus insuring that the chain will curve in and out and around all the cogs and pulley wheels in the rear cage.

We assume that when you tracked the frame you checked the rear ends (dropouts). These should of course, be parallel and the gear hanger likewise.

Should the right hand end be fitted with one, Campagnolo issues a testing rod, and if your workshop is equipped with this useful article, by all means be sure that you use it.

It consists of a threaded part which screws into the hanger and a gauge which will tell you if the hanger is square to the chain line.

In case the reader is unacquainted with the difference between dropouts with or without a gear hanger, perhaps we had better explain.

Derailleur gears have to be attached to the rear dropouts. In the majority of cases this is accomplished by a bracket which is attached to the gear system pivot, and the other end of bracket is bolted to the rear fork end. This insures that the gear stays in position when the wheel is removed.

The other method is to make the bracket part and parcel of the dropout. This appears as a large threaded eyelet below the fork end, the pivot bolt of the gear screwing into this attachment.

Campagnolo and Simplex are two firms who make forkends so equipped. These dropouts usually have provisions for adjusters which will have spring loaded screws.

The idea here is that when the wheel is located in the fork ends in the best position for maximum gear working efficiency, the adjusters are tightened up to rest against the axle. In the event of wheel removal, the wheel can be reinstalled simply by pulling it back until the axle touches the adjusters.

Apart from the different makes of gears, each make generally has at least two types: One for close ratios and the other for a wider range of gears. The latter is normally used for touring.

The touring type gear can readily be distinguished from

the close ratio pattern by one of two things. It will either have a longer cage or will be of the double springing variety. With a close ratio cluster the teeth step up is usually one or two teeth difference, so that a normal gear changer is adequate.

However, the Huret Allivet, an excellent gear that is moderately priced, will handle rear clusters from about 14 to 30 teeth.

Likewise the Simplex Prestige, a double springed gear, is also used on most types of clusters.

The main idea of course is that no matter how many teeth or how few on each cog—the chain should have maximum wrap-around. This means that the chain should engage as many teeth as possible to avoid slipping.

Chain tension is another important feature. But of course it is no use to have a nice tight chain on the small high cog if that tightness does not allow the chain to climb up smoothly on to the large cog.

This of course follows with the front sprocket set-up—again a close ratio, two teeth or so difference between the rings does not give the same problems as would an "Alpine-Gear" arrangement.

The chain should be long enough so that when running on the large front sprocket, it will just climb up onto the large rear cog without strain.

This again will insure that when the smaller cogs are engaged the chain is not too loose and combined with the correct tension will not slip.

Some gears will be found to have apart from the two adjusting screws that give inner and outer lateral control, a third adjusting screw which controls the distance of the guide roller (the top cage roller) from the cluster.

This should be judged carefully. In other words, it would all be very well bringing the guide roller nice and close to the small cog on the cluster to give a good wrap-around.

But how about engaging the large inside cog? Chances are

that the gear cage will foul it.

To be sure, some cages like the "Huret Allivet" rise and fall, following the contour of the cluster; but these points should be carefully checked.

The gear cage should be parallel to the cluster when viewed from above. Whether your control wires are of the bare variety or the kind that are encased all the way with sleeving, make sure they are free from kinks, both inner and outer.

Also, be sure to keep the inner wire lightly greased.

Make sure that the levers move freely and that all washers, spacers, spring caps, etc., are in the correct order and are centered.

One frequently finds left hand levers mounted on the right and vice versa, and pressure plates on the slant with one part of the center hole resting on the boss shoulder.

If this is neglected and the damper wing-nut is tightened, it is easy to see that the plate gets distorted. Screws and dampers should be finger tightened only, otherwise the spring cup will get flattened and the gear lever will be so tight that it will become impossible to move, or else you will not be able to get any form of tightness.

When inspecting the front changer, make sure it is parallel to the front sprocket or sprockets.

If they are not parallel, unscrew one or both bolts on the clamp that holds it to the frame tube and twist into line, making sure of course, that it is not just the cage that is bent.

If the latter, see whether or not you can straighten it—sometimes they are too far gone—in which case a new one is the only answer.

Check the inside of the cage for any wear, scars, etc. Many times the machine will have been ridden for quite a long time with the front changer out of adjustment—resulting in chain wear.

If not too excessive, take a file and carefully smooth down the metal.

The inside must be free from any burrs or abrasions,

otherwise smooth changing can never be accomplished.

The height of the front changer is another important factor to be observed—in other words the distance between the changer and teeth of the sprocket.

Under normal conditions, the closer the better. But when the chain is on the small rear cog and outside the large front sprocket and is running fine, it does not mean that the same smooth action will be found when we switch to the rear large cog. This will alter the angle of the chain when viewed from the side, resulting possibly in the chain rubbing on the inside part of the top of the changer cage.

Some manufacturers will give measurements regarding this distance, but experience will tell you to use this as a guide as the exact measurement is not always possible.

Returning to the rear gear system, it is possible on some occasions to extend the number of teeth on the large rear cog without installing a new and different gear.

For example, on a Huret Allvit if we install a thin shim-washer with a tongue on it between the pivot bracket and main assembly, this will prevent the system from going forward too much as the tongue engages between the two stops.

Another measure that you can use in extreme circumstances is to build up the shoulder stop on the hanger with a little brass.

If we do this we must check to see that the small cog (high gear) still has enough wrap around, otherwise slippage will result.

Of course, as stated previously, we are speaking of borderline cases: With really wide ratios a long cage touring or a double springing gear is the answer.

I remember some years ago a favorite trick of mine was to take a Campagnolo Sport which has the springing action at the top pivot point, knock out the rivets, then to take a Gran Sport Campagnolo, knock out these rivets at the top, and re-rivet, combining the springing actions of both gears. This enabled those whose favorite gear was a Campagnolo to increase their gear range without having to buy a touring gear of a different make.

The Nuovo Record and Tourismo gears were not available in those days when I worked on them.

Let us now try a little trouble-shooting. On the rear gear system, if the chain does not go on to the large inside cog, check cable wire. If too slack, tighten, if very slight, use cable adjuster.

If excessive, undo the anchor bolt assembly and pull wire barely taut.. (Do this when chain is on small cog).

Note that some gears have a bolt with a hole, some a shouldered bolt that relies on a tongued-washer. The latter is also used in conjunction with the grooved bolt.

Whatever style is used, be sure without overtightening, that the wire is gripped securely.

If the chain still does not climb up—do not strain the cable—Check the inward adjusting screw, but do not be too eager. Unscrew a little at a time.

If this still does not do the trick, make sure the plates of the cage on each side of the roller are not bent out. If they are, gently pull them in. The outer one can even be pulled up a little closer.

This will give the chain just that little impetus needed, but do not overdo it.

We have already stressed the importance of having the cage parallel to the cluster.

If this is out, make sure it is the cage and not the body of the gear—carefully straighten by using either the special tool or the adjustable wrench.

In some cases for example, a twisted "Huret Allvit" body can be straightened by gripping the bottom pivoting bolt on each side with the vise grip—in which case you will find that you have an excellent purchase.

Penultimately, if you still can not get the large cog, check the lever.

Today levers are mounted in so many different positions and places that they do not always have the full radius they used to have when mounted on the down tube of the frame.

A case in point is the Schwinn twin or single-stick control which is situated under the top nut right by the gooseneck.

I have found that it is sometimes necessary to remove a little metal from the tongue of the pressure-washer.

This will enable the lever to have a greater traverse. Be careful not to take too much off, otherwise, the lever can come down too far and foul the top tube.

Finally, or perhaps before you try this last adjustment, we should have checked the axle spacing. If excessive this will curtail the throw of the gear.

We are of course, referring to the spacer on the axle at the small cog end of the cluster.

This can be comprised of a sleeve, sometimes threaded, sometimes not, with an additional washer and lock nut. It will be found that by just removing the washer it will be enough to make all the difference.

One last word. If the cage or roller fouls the large cog, we refer you to the earlier notes in this chapter.

Having now adjusted the gear to climb up smoothly onto the large cog—we find that it does not want to engage the smallest cog.

First, check the outward adjusting screw and unscrew as is necessary.

Check to see that when we tightened the gear wire we did not overdo it.

Next check the pivoting pins in the cage. If as in the Huret Allvit, they are bolts, unscrew the nuts, back off the bolts, and then retighten the nuts.

If riveted, spray well with WD 40 or L.P.S. and work it backwards and forwards with your hand, taking the chain off from the front sprocket, to release tension.

In extreme circumstances replace the spring.

If the gear was bent and we have straightened it, check to

see that the inner members of the cage are not distorted. That is, that they catch on each other instead of just passing.

Our former remarks about the cage case hold good also for the small adjustment.

Another point that sometimes influences the lining up of gears are the rollers. These must be free to rotate, but any side play must be taken up.

The rollers can be either ball-bearing or a form of plastic with center steel bushings, a dust cap each side running in canalures completing the set-up.

If too worn to be adjusted satisfactorily—replace.

It is a good idea to keep old twisted and broken gears. They will often have rollers in good condition and in these present times of spare parts shortage, they can come in mighty handy as replacements.

Let us return to the front changer and do a little trouble-shooting here.

If difficulty in changing gears is experienced, check the cage positioning over the front chainwheels making sure that the cage is the correct height and parallel.

Now set the chain on the large inside rear cog and on the front inside small cog.

The cage should be over the center of the small cog with no tension on the left hand gear wire or lever.

If we depart from this positioning it would be to bring the cage slightly towards the large front cog; this would be carried out if the chain persists in dropping down on the inside—between the front sprockets and the seat tube.

Again, we must assume that you have checked sprockets for truth and alignment with rear cluster.

Check to see that the inside adjusting screw is set to limit this position or as in some front changers the cage holding clamp is also the inside adjuster. Put the chain down on the rear small cog and try the front—Will it climb up onto the large front cog? No?

O.K. Let us check to see that the wire is not sagging.

In other words, when we move the lever it takes time before the cage starts to move.

If loose, tighten the wire and be careful not to overtighten as we do not want to influence the inside sprocket adjustment.

Now check the outward throw adjusting screw and let us try again.

The chain climbs up now, but also goes right over. If so, we undid the adjusting screw a little too much.

Now replace the chain, screw the adjuster back a little and try again.

When once it seems to work O.K. go through all the gears vigourously and repeat several times.

Please remember that the rider is not always going to change gears slowly and carefully, so you should allow for this factor.

In certain circumstances it is permissable to bend slightly the inside of the front cage to assist in smarter gear changing.

Common sense and patience are the two important factors with all derailleur installations and adjustments.

To further assist the reader we are listing some of the more popular gears, showing the adjusting points and noting the teeth capacities.

It must be observed that to describe every gear, as well as other components in this manual is virtually impossible. To do this would require a set of books.

We can not leave this chapter without mentioning the Japanese company of Shimano whose splendid range of derailleurs covers all phases of bicycling.

Shimano Lark and Eagle derailleurs are double springing; they are sensibly priced to fill the needs of the average cyclist. For more discerning enthusiasts the Shimano Crane derailleur, one of many components in their excellent Dura-Ace series, is manufactured from "micra-alloy" metal to combine maximum strength and lightness with a fine finish — weight: 7.9 oz., capacity: 28 tooth difference.

SHIMANO

Derailleurs

Crane G.S.

Model No.: D510
Capacity: 34 teeth
Weight: 9.5 oz (270g)
Material: Light Alloy
Without Adaptor: (Model No. D511)

Eagle S.S.

Model No.. D310
Capacity: 34 teeth
Weight: 13.4 oz (380g)
Material: Steel
With Cable Saver and
Derailleur Guard

SIMPLEX CONTROL LEVER SPARE PARTS

CYCLO'S GEAR CHART. 26" & 27" WHEELS

CHAIN WHEEL	24th		26th		28th		30th		32th		34th		36th		38th		40th		42th		44th	
WHEEL SIZE / sprocket size	26in	27in	26in	27in	26in	27in	26in	27in	26in	27in	26in	27in	26in	27in	26in	27in	26in	27in	26in	27in	26in	27in
12	52.1	54.1	56.3	58.5	60.6	63.0	65.0	67.5	69.2	72.0	73.8	76.5	78.0	81.1	82.4	85.5	86.7	90.0	91.0	94.5	95.3	99.0
13	48.0	49.8	52.0	54.0	56.0	58.1	60.0	62.3	64.1	66.4	68.0	70.6	72.0	74.7	76.0	78.9	80.0	83.1	84.0	87.2	88.0	91.4
14	44.7	46.2	48.2	50.1	52.0	54.0	55.7	57.8	59.5	61.7	63.1	65.5	66.8	69.5	70.6	73.3	74.3	77.1	78.0	81.0	81.7	84.9
15	41.6	43.2	45.0	46.8	48.5	50.4	52.0	54.0	55.6	57.6	59.0	61.1	62.4	64.8	65.9	68.4	69.3	72.0	72.8	75.6	76.3	79.2
16	39.1	40.5	42.2	43.7	45.5	47.2	48.7	50.6	52.0	54.0	55.2	57.2	58.5	60.9	61.8	64.1	65.0	67.5	68.3	70.9	71.5	74.3
17	36.7	38.1	39.7	41.2	42.8	44.4	45.8	47.6	49.0	50.8	52.0	54.0	55.0	57.2	58.1	60.3	61.2	63.5	64.2	66.7	67.3	69.9
18	34.6	36.0	37.5	39.0	40.5	42.0	43.3	45.0	46.2	48.0	49.2	51.0	52.0	54.0	54.9	57.0	57.8	60.0	60.6	63.0	63.6	66.0
19	32.9	34.1	35.5	36.8	38.3	39.7	41.0	42.6	43.8	45.5	46.5	48.2	49.2	51.1	52.0	54.0	54.7	56.8	57.5	59.7	60.2	62.5
20	31.2	32.4	33.8	35.1	36.4	37.8	39.0	40.5	41.6	43.2	44.2	45.9	46.7	48.7	49.4	51.3	52.0	54.0	54.6	56.7	57.2	59.4
21	29.7	30.8	32.1	33.4	34.6	36.0	37.1	38.6	39.7	41.1	42.0	43.7	44.5	46.4	46.1	48.9	49.5	51.4	52.0	54.0	54.5	56.6
22	28.4	29.4	30.7	31.9	33.0	34.3	35.4	36.8	37.9	39.2	40.2	41.6	42.5	44.2	44.9	46.6	47.3	49.1	49.6	51.5	52.0	54.0
23	27.1	28.1	29.3	30.5	31.6	32.8	33.9	35.2	36.2	37.5	38.4	39.9	40.6	42.4	43.0	44.6	45.2	47.0	47.5	49.3	49.8	51.6
24	26.0	27.0	28.1	29.2	30.3	31.5	32.5	33.7	34.7	36.0	36.8	38.2	39.0	40.5	41.2	42.8	43.3	45.0	45.5	47.3	47.7	49.5
25	25.0	25.9	27.0	28.0	29.1	30.2	31.2	32.4	33.4	34.6	35.4	36.7	37.4	38.9	39.5	41.0	41.6	43.2	43.7	45.4	45.8	47.5
26	24.1	24.9	26.0	27.0	28.0	29.0	30.0	31.2	32.8	33.2	34.0	35.3	36.0	37.4	38.0	39.5	40.0	41.5	42.0	43.6	44.0	45.7
28	22.3	23.1	24.1	25.0	26.0	27.0	27.8	28.9	29.7	30.8	31.6	32.8	33.4	34.8	35.3	36.6	37.1	38.6	39.0	40.5	40.9	42.4

CHAIN WHEEL	45th		46th		47th		48th		49th		50th		52nd		53rd		54th		55th		56th	
WHEEL SIZE	26in	27in	26in	27in	26in	27in	26in	27in	26in	27in	26in	27in	26in	27in	26in	27in	26in	27in	26in	27in	26in	27in
sprocket size																						
12	97·5	101·2	99·7	103·5	101·8	105·7	104·0	108·0	106·1	110·2	108·3	112·3	112·7	117·0	114·8	119·3	117·0	121·5	119·1	123·7	121·3	126·0
13	90·0	93·4	92·0	95·5	94·0	97·6	96·0	99·7	98·0	101·8	100·0	103·9	104·0	108·0	106·0	110·0	108·0	112·1	110·0	114·2	112·0	116·3
14	83·5	86·7	85·4	88·7	87·3	90·6	89·1	92·6	91·0	94·5	92·9	96·4	96·6	100·3	98·4	102·2	100·3	104·1	102·1	106·0	104·0	108·0
15	78·0	80·9	79·7	82·8	81·5	84·6	83·2	86·4	84·9	88·2	86·7	90·0	90·1	93·6	91·8	95·4	93·6	97·2	95·3	99·0	97·0	100·8
16	73·1	76·0	74·6	77·6	76·4	79·3	78·0	81·0	79·6	82·7	81·3	84·4	84·5	87·8	86·1	89·4	87·7	91·1	89·3	92·8	91·0	94·5
17	68·8	71·5	70·4	73·1	71·9	74·6	73·4	76·2	74·9	77·8	76·5	79·4	79·5	82·6	81·0	84·1	82·5	85·7	84·1	87·3	85·6	88·9
18	65·0	67·5	66·4	69·0	67·9	70·5	69·3	72·0	70·7	73·5	72·2	75·0	75·1	78·0	76·5	79·5	78·0	81·0	79·4	82·5	80·8	84·0
19	61·7	64·0	62·9	65·4	64·3	66·8	65·7	68·2	67·0	69·6	68·4	71·1	71·2	73·9	72·5	75·3	73·9	76·7	75·2	78·1	76·6	79·5
20	58·5	60·8	59·8	62·1	61·1	63·4	62·4	64·8	63·7	66·2	65·0	67·5	67·6	70·2	68·9	71·5	70·2	72·9	71·5	74·5	72·8	75·6
21	55·8	57·9	57·0	59·1	58·2	60·4	59·4	61·7	60·6	63·0	61·9	64·3	64·4	66·9	65·6	68·1	66·8	69·4	68·0	70·7	69·3	72·0
22	53·1	55·2	54·4	56·5	55·5	57·6	56·7	58·9	57·9	60·1	59·1	61·4	61·5	63·8	62·6	65·0	63·8	66·2	65·0	67·5	66·1	68·7
23	50·8	52·8	52·0	54·0	53·1	55·2	54·3	56·3	55·4	57·5	56·5	58·7	58·8	61·0	59·9	62·2	61·0	63·6	62·1	64·5	63·3	65·7
24	48·6	50·7	49·9	51·8	50·9	52·9	52·0	54·0	53·1	55·1	54·2	56·3	56·3	58·5	57·4	59·6	58·5	60·7	59·5	61·8	60·6	63·0
25	46·9	48·6	47·8	49·7	48·9	50·8	49·9	51·8	51·0	52·9	52·0	54·0	54·1	56·2	55·1	57·2	56·1	58·3	57·2	59·4	58·2	60·4
26	45·0	46·7	46·0	47·8	47·0	48·8	48·0	49·9	49·0	50·9	50·0	51·9	52·0	54·0	53·0	55·0	54·0	56·0	55·0	57·1	56·0	58·1
28	41·8	43·4	42·7	44·4	43·6	45·3	44·6	46·3	45·5	47·2	46·4	48·2	48·3	50·1	49·2	51·1	50·1	52·0	51·0	53·0	52·0	54·0

CYCLO GEAR CO. LTD., BIRMINGHAM, 6, ENGLAND

HURET
SUPER
ALLVIT

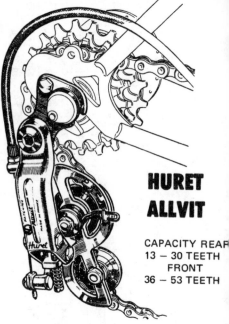

SVELTO

HURET
ALLVIT

CAPACITY REAR
13 — 24 TEETH
FRONT
36 — 53 TEETH

CAPACITY REAR
13 — 30 TEETH
FRONT
36 — 53 TEETH

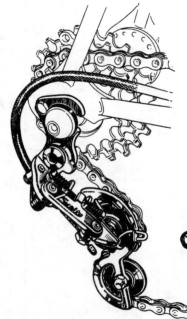

No. 600 FRONT
SHIFTER
ASSEMBLY

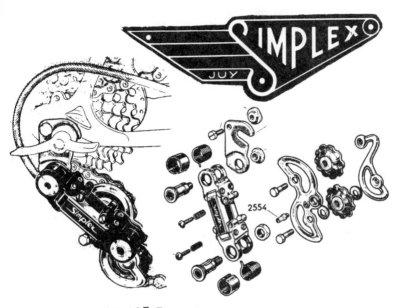

PRESTIGE **AR** 537 **P**

PRESTIGE MODEL 537/P
Supplied with bracket Ref. 2645
to fit standard type rear FORKEND ONLY.

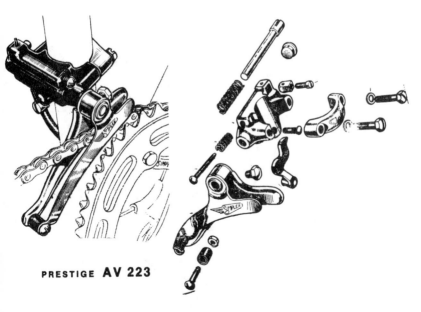

PRESTIGE **AV 223**

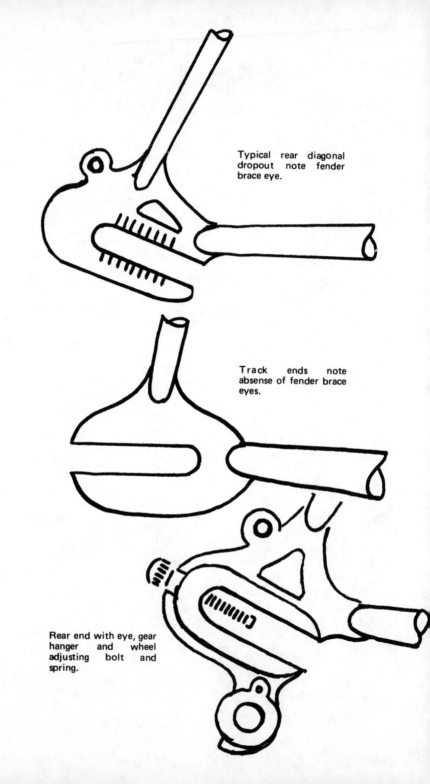

Typical rear diagonal dropout note fender brace eye.

Track ends note absense of fender brace eyes.

Rear end with eye, gear hanger and wheel adjusting bolt and spring.

8

HUB GEARS

In the previous chapter of this manual, we cover the derailleur system of variable gearing.

In this chapter we need to look at the type of gear which is contained within the rear hub, namely, the "epicyclic gear."

This in brief consists of a central gear or pinion which is usually known as the sun pinion. This does not rotate itself, but it has a series of pinions, known as planets rotating around it.

Surrounding the planet is an internally toothed ring that is known as the gear ring or annulus, and is generally equipped with two pawls which are actuated by springs.

The planets themselves rotate on pins which are supported in a planet cage; the lower portion of which is also equipped with two spring-loaded pawls.

The sun pinion is part and parcel of the axle and is fitted with a sliding clutch which in turn is attached to the driver and cog.

This entire assembly is mounted inside the hub shell. The hub shell is fitted at each end with a ratchet formed ball cup.

When in high gear, drive is from sprocket to planet pinion spindle. The planet rolls around the fixed sun pinion. The outside of the planet moves faster and this drives the gear ring which in turn is connected to the hub.

When in normal gear, drive is from sprocket direct to gear ring to hub shell. The planets in this case rotate idly around the sun pinion.

Lastly, when in low or bottom gear, drive is from sprocket to gear ring. This rotates planets around sun pinion, and the planet pinion spindles move slower than the gear ring.

These spindles are coupled through the planet cage to the hub shell. All of these operations are carried out by manipulating the sliding clutch, which engages either the top of the protruding pinion pins or the dogs on the inner surface of the gear ring.

The sliding clutch also allows the pawls on the gearing to operate or throws them out of commission.

Before dismantling any variable geared hub we should always check the cable adjustment. Do this by examining the indicator rod and set it depending on the model of the hub.

The cable wire should be checked to see that it is free from kinks and runs smoothly in its casing. Always keep it lubricated with a thin coating of grease.

Make sure that the control is working correctly. If the wire goes over a pulley wheel, check to see that this rotates freely.

A great mistake that a lot of riders make is to use the brake cable clips to also hold the inner wire of the gear down.

This does not affect the gear so much when pulling through, for example, from top to bottom, but when you want to return to the top, the clips do not allow free travel of the wire.

Another thing to check is the control or trigger. The nut and bolt that holds it in place on the handlebar passes through the body of the control—overtightening of this bolt can lead to sluggish trigger action.

By far the best and most popular 3-speed hub in use, is the Sturmey Archer A.W. hub made by the Raleigh Bicycle Co. Simple and sweet, it has no equal.

Imitation is the most sincere form of flattery and the Hercules company before it merged with Raleigh brought out a copy. Likewise, the Armstrong company, and Steyr of Austria have also issued a copy.

With the exception of the Hercules, where the pinion pins were of a slightly different thickness, all parts of these hubs are interchangeable.

Since the hubs introduction in 1937, various modifications

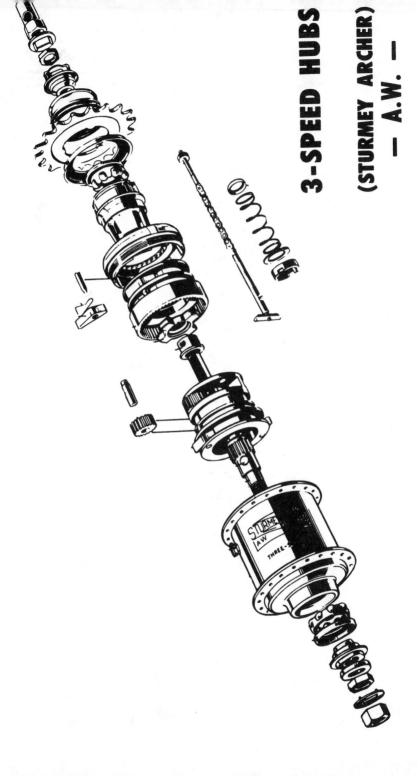

3-SPEED HUBS

(STURMEY ARCHER)
— A.W. —

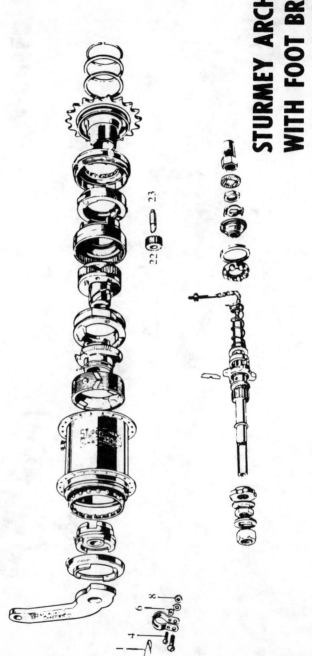

STURMEY ARCHER
WITH FOOT BRAKE
T.C.W. 3 SPEED

have taken place. The only one we have to be concerned about is the left-hand ball cup. This used to be threaded into the hub and had flats on the outside for wrench or vise usage.

Today the cup has a smooth exterior and is pressed into the hub. Let us take one of these famous hubs to pieces.

Using the flat surfaces of the axle to hold it in the vise, remove the left-hand locknut and cone; likewise any washers, checking their order for correct reassembly.

Remove cog from driver, noting position of offset or bell shape and where the washers are located. All of these control the chain line.

Use a thin screwdriver to pry off the snap-ring. Earlier models used threaded driver and cog. In this case the cog can only be removed with the driver out of hub and held by a special tool.

If you do not have the tool, slip a piece of steel thick enough for the legs of the driver to mount over in the vise, and using your chain stick unscrew counter-clockwise. With a hammer and drift punch, unscrew the right-hand ball cup.

This has two notches and unscrews counter-clockwise. Now you can remove the whole of the internals as a unit.

In the case of the hub shell having a two start thread, it is a good idea to put a piece of adhesive tape on the spoke adjacent to one of the notches.

When you reassemble you will know that you have the cup back in the same position. Failure to do this could mean retruing of the wheel should you have used the wrong thread.

Place the axle horizontally with the left-hand end in the vise.

Now we can remove the right-hand lock-nut, washer and cone. They unscrew counter-clockwise.

If any additional washers are fitted, note their sequence so that they can be replaced in the same order. Remove driver, clutch, spring, the right-hand cup and the gear ring.

Remove the thrust ring, and washer if in two parts. Unscrew the indicator rod and chain.

Now push out the axle key sideways and take off the sliding clutch and sleeve (the last named is shaped after the style of a top hat). Lift off the planet cage and take out the planets and pins.

If we have to remove the pawls from the gear ring or from the planet cage, it is a good idea to do them one at a time. In this way, when replacing we can use the other side as a pattern.

The dust caps are pressed in and can be removed carefully in the usual manner with a thin screwdriver.

The caps in the left-hand ball cup and driver go in with the open parts facing outward. This is for the dust caps on the cones to fit into and form a seal.

Lay all the parts out on the bench and check the following:

The sliding clutch which should slide up and down easily in the driver. When mounted on the sleeve, it should slide up and down on the axle.

Check the axle for straightness. Inspect all teeth on the pinions and gear ring for wear or chipping.

Examine all six race surfaces for wear and pitting. Check sliding clutch, gear ring dogs and tops of pinion pins for rounding off where they are engaged by the clutch.

We come now to the reassembling of the hub.

If we have removed the left-hand ball cup from the hub, replace it. It threads into the shell counter-clockwise. If it is of the splined variety, tap it back into place. Use a block of wood to soften the force of the hammer.

Replace the pawls in the gear ring. If we find that we have taken the pawls from both sides of this component and therefore can not use one as a pattern, proceed as follows:

Place a spring by the side of the pawl so that the looped part is over the pin hole and the foot is under the long part of the pawl.

Hold a pawl pin handy in the left-hand as you grip the foot of the spring and long part of the pawl between the finger and thumb of the other hand.

Now slide the pawl with the other end first between the ledges of the gear ring.

When the holes in the gear ring line up with the hole in the pawl and the loop in the spring, place the pawl pin in position.

Check the springing action several times and oil the pivotal point with Raleigh oil.

Now grease the ball retainer bearing surfaces in the left-hand ball cup, driver and the bearing channel in the right-hand ball cup. These are the only places that we use grease, and the rest of the internals must run in oil.

Place the axle in vise in the same position that we adopted for dismantling.

Install the planet cage so that the sun pinion is inside and the slot in axle is on the outside of planet cage.

Next, place the four pinions and their pins in place with the small ends protruding.

Now, fit the clutch sleeve (top hat) flange first, followed by the clutch so that the recess fits over the sleeve flange.

With the flats outward, fit the axle key and thrust ring so that the flats engage the two notches. If the thrust ring takes a washer, install this next.

Screw in the indicator rod and chain. This will hold the key in position while we are assembling the rest of the hub.

Now place the gearing over the planet cage, making sure that it seats correctly. The right-hand ball cup comes next.

If we have removed the dust cap and balls, we can replace these into the grease filled bearing recess. This takes 24 3/16" balls.

Tap the dust caps over lightly, making sure the balls can rotate easily.

With the ball retainer and dust cap fitted, install the driver.

Now, place the clutch spring over the axle. Note that some hubs are fitted with a spring cap which goes over the end of the spring and is engaged by the right-hand cone. This will go on the axle next.

Screw this up finger tight and then back off half a turn. Using the "U" shaped washer and lock-nut, lock it in place.

Never unscrew this cone back more than this, otherwise, it will throw the rest of the gear out of adjustment.

Take the gear assembly out of the vise and, if we have removed the planet pawls, place the right-hand end of the axle in the vise. Naturally we will grip it by the flats so that the assembly is vertical.

In order to install the pawls, place a pawl between the ledger of the planet cage with the flat edge pointing to the right. Insert a pawl pin into the outside ledge and halfway into the pawl.

With a pair of tweezers hold the bent part of the spring; and pass the spring under the pawl until the loop of the spring coincides with the hole in the pawl, and both ends of the spring are in between the pawl and cage.

Now push home the pin and try the action of the pawl several times.

Finally, make sure that the internals are well oiled before we insert the internal assembly into the shell.

While you hold the shell in the left hand, grasp the gear assembly in the right by the right-hand ball cup and screw into place.

Check to see whether the notches line up with our marked spoke, and with the punch and hammer lock the right-hand ball cup tight.

Install the left-hand cone and washers and lock-nut, and then adjust hub in the usual manner. Just in case we have forgotten how to do it, we will need a cone wrench to hold the cone and an adjustable wrench with which to lock it.

The hub should now rotate freely without side shake. Replace the cog and washers in correct sequence in the same order they were in before we dismantled them.

When installing our three-speed wheel, care should be taken to see that the axle does not turn in the rear fork ends.

This can be prevented by using the special eared washers. These fit on the axle flats with the ears fitting in the fork end slots.

If the ends have 5/16" openings, these washers are not needed. I always like to use a good pair of serrated washers under the nuts.

Always make sure that our indicator rod and chain is screwed into the axle fully and backed off just sufficiently to line it up with the control wire. It is important to remember that we never unscrew it more than half a turn.

When the control triggers give trouble they are generally past the repairing stage and should be replaced.

Twist grips, on the other hand, in the main last longer and apart from replacing the ball and spring require only a little lubrication from time to time to keep them operating.

The Sturmey Archer three-speed hubs with coaster brakes have similar gear ratios to the A.W. Sturmey Archer, but they also have brakes incorporated in the hub. There are three main types that will be encountered.

Sturmey Archer T.C.W. (1952-1959) and the S.A. T.C.W. (1959-1961). Both of these are interchangeable with each other—they can therefore be classed as one type.

The second type is the Sturmey Archer T.C.W. (1959-1961). This is the hub that the mechanic is most likely to find himself working with.

Finally, the latest type of 3-speed gear combined with a coaster brake is the S.3C.

As this writer has not yet had the opportunity to work on one, we hesitate to give you more on it at this time. In our next edition of *THE BICYCLE MANUAL* we will include other models and accessories, etc. that are not covered in this book.

Let us now have a look at the original T.C.W. (1952-1959) and the subsequent (1959-1961) type.

When you remove the sprocket, as per earlier instructions (I have not come in contact with any hub of this pattern with

OLD STYLE TCW HUB PARTS
Not Interchangeable with Mark 3 TCW

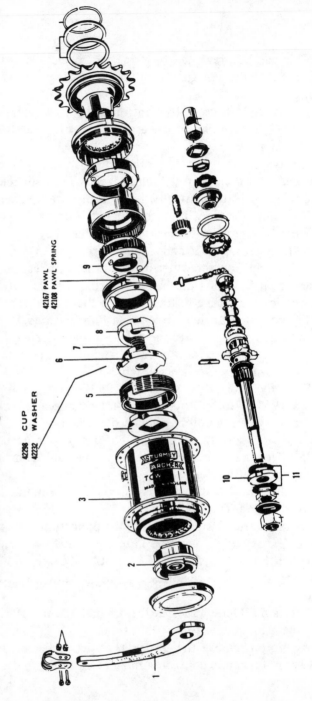

42167 PAWL
42108 PAWL SPRING

4298 CUP
4232 WASHER

ART REF.	MFG. PART NO.	DESCRIPTION
①	K-495	BRAKE ARM
②	K-494	Left hand cone
③	K-492Z	Shell, 40 hole with ball cup
③	K-429AZ	Shell, 36 hole with ball cup
④	HSH-414	Brake plate
⑤	HSH-413	Brake band
	HSH-416	Thrust cup
	HMW-162	Thrust washer
⑥	HSH-412	Brake thrust plate
⑦	HSA-212	Spring
⑧	HSH-411	Brake cam
	HSA-111	Low gear pawl
	HSA-120	Pawl spring
⑨	HSH-409	Planet cage
⑩	K-496	Brake arm nut
⑪	HMW-350	Washer

threaded drivers) do not forget to check the sequence of washers and which way the offset cog was installed.

Put the hub in the vise, gripping flats of axle, on the sprocket side.

With a "C" type of spanner holding cone adjusting nut, undo the outer lock-nut. Use a crescent wrench or 15 mm cone wrench.

Next, remove these pieces, together with the two lock washers. Please take note again of their sequence. Take off brake arm and dust cap from brake arm cone.

Remove the hub from vise and with a drift punch and hammer undo the right-hand ball cup, using the same procedure as for an A.W. hub, counter-clockwise.

Rotate both brake arm cone and right-hand ball cup until right-hand cup is loose from shell.

Take off brake arm cone and remove right-hand cup and hub internals from shell as a unit.

Put the axle with sprocket side in vise. Take off brake plate (expander) and brass brake band.

Next remove brake thrust plate followed by the short spring. Note that for hubs (1959-1961) a longer spring was used, together with a different thrust plate. A spring cap and friction washer was another addition at that time.

Now we can remove low gear pawl ring and brake cam. If pawls are worn and the springs are weak, proceed as follows:

Using a thin screwdriver, pry pawl spring around bottom corner of pawl and remove. The pawl pins are riveted and have to be drilled out, should removal be necessary.

Reverse the axle assembly in vise to remove lock-nut, washer cone, driver, right-hand ball cup, the gear ring pawl ring and the gear ring.

Take off clutch spring, thrust ring, or washer and ring, should they be seperate. Unscrew the indicator rod and chain if you have not already removed them. Push out the axle key and remove clutch and sleeve.

Remove the pinion pins and take out the pinions. All that

remains is the planet cage which just lifts off the axle.

The left-hand ball cup is pressed into the hub shell and it is not advisable to attempt to remove it. If worn or pitted it is replaceable with the hub shell as one unit. Both right and left ball cups take 24 3/16" loose balls and are held in place with a press-on dust cap.

We will enumerate the parts to inspect and check:

(1) Sliding clutch—it should be free in driver to slide up and down.

(2) Axle—it should not be bent.

(3) Gear teeth—they should all be free from wear and chipping.

(4) Races, six in all—they should all be free from wear and pitting.

(5) Pinion pins, clutch and gear ring dogs—they should not be rounded off where they engage their opposite number.

(6) Pawl and ratchets—they should not be worn.

(7) Pawl rings—they should not be cracked around rivets.

(8) Brake band or cylinder—they should not be smooth or have a glazed look.

(9) Threaded parts—they should not be stripped.

When assembling, place axle in vise, gripping by the flats with slot uppermost.

Install planet cage on axle so that it seats correctly on the sun pinion.

Position planet pinions in cage. Secure them in place with the planet pins, making sure that the flats are pointing down.

Next comes the top hat shaped sleeve. Make sure that you align sleeve holes with the axle slot.

Now install the clutch so that the four arms fit between the pinion pins. Do not forget that the bottom of the clutch is recessed to fit over the brim of the top hat sleeve.

Now insert the axle key with flats facing upward. Install thrust ring and washer (if in two parts) locating the notches with the key flats.

Now lower the clutch spring and cap (if one is used). If

hub is the type that uses the long brake side spring, do not mix them up. In this case the shorter of the two would be the clutch spring.

Next comes the gear ring followed by the gear pawl ring. If we have removed pawls or springs, see notes at end of the assembly instructions.

If fitted correctly, the gear ring pawl ring should have the heads of the pawl pins facing upwards. Rotate this assembly a few times to make sure gear ring is meshing correctly with the pinions in the planet cage.

Now install the right-hand ball cup depressing pawls on gear ring pawl ring until ball cup locates correctly on gear ring.

Please note that if any balls were missing from ball cups be sure to replace the lot, 24 in number.

After smearing the ball channel with grease and replacing dust cap, the latter should be tapped gently in place with the ball cup resting on the bench.

Making sure that our ball cage is in good condition and greased, install the driver, twisting back and forth so that the driver slots fit over the clutch.

Now we can screw on the right-hand cone, finger-tight and then back off approximately 1/2 turn.

Install the "U" shaped washer so that the ears engage the flats on the cone. Do not unscrew cone more than another 1/4 turn to do this.

Now install and tighten down the lock-nut. At this point rotate the assembly back and forth again to double check that all parts are seated and meshing correctly. Reverse axle assembly in vise.

To install planet cage pawl ring, make sure the flats on planet pins are facing outward and lower pawl ring with the two legs facing outwards.

Now lower over axle the brake cam so that the cavities fit over the ends of the planet pins. If of the short spring variety gently stretch the spring before installing it.

Follow this with the brake thrust plate taking care that the two slots fit over the legs of the planet cage gearing. The smallest part of the tapered sides should be on top.

If of the long spring type—a good tip after installing the spring, spring caps and washer is to compress the spring.

Do this using a steel sleeve (the fixing sleeve from an old A.W. hub can be used), place this over the axle and secure with the normal outer lock-nut.

Now install the brake band with slot facing outwards.

Next fit the brake plate or expander with the tapered part pointing downwards. The key should fit into the brake band slot.

Making sure the 24 3/16" balls are grease packed in the left-hand ball cups and the dust cap is tapped home, we can now install the internals.

Remove the assembly from vise. Holding it by the right-hand ball cup, driver side at bottom and in right-hand, guide it up into the hub shell which you will be holding in the left hand.

Place brake arm cone in the left-hand ball cup, making sure to align the square part with the hole in the brake plate or expander.

Now rotate the right hand ball cup and brake arm cone to the left to seat the planet cage pawls in left-hand ball cup. When you hear them click into place screw home tightly the right-hand ball cup up against the hub shell.

When assembling the T.C.W. hub with the long retarder spring set, please remember that we have the sleeve and lock-nut compressing the spring. Do not install the left-hand cone.

After we have tightened down the right-hand ball cup with this pattern hub, remove lock-nut and sleeve and then we can install left-hand cone followed by the dust cap and brake arm.

The brake arm should fit tightly in the slots and in some cases it will be found necessary to tap it in place with a hammer. Now replace washer and cone adjuster followed by washer and lock-nut.

Now we use our "C" spanner to hold the cone adjusting nut while we tighten down the outer lock-nut. Check the adjustment.

In this type of hub, you nearly always have to leave a trace of play. If too tight slacken off outer lock-nut and then the cone adjusting nut. Again hold the cone adjusting nut and tighten down the outer nut.

We will quote the manufacturer on how to replace pawls and springs in the planet cage pawl ring:

"Fit pawl spring ring and pin as shown in diagram 1. Support the pawl pin head on a piece of flat steel held in a vise. The pawl pin must be riveted over lightly and without distorting the pin head, which can cause serious damage if it projects inwards".

"To replace pawls and springs in gear ring pawl ring, first fit a pawl pin into the pawl ring as shown in diagram 11 and rivet the pawl pin into position."

"File the pawl pin end so that it does not project beyond the face of the pawl ring."

"Turn the pawl back as far as it will go, and insert the tail of the spring between the pawl ring. At the same time the bent end of the spring should be fitted under the shorter end of the pawl."

"Then turn back the pawl to its correct position."

The main difference between the Sturmey Archer T.C.W. Mark 3 three-speed hub and its predecessors is on the brake arm side. This is not to say that you can interchange all the other parts. The axle for one thing is different.

To dismantle you would proceed as with the other Sturmey Archer hubs by placing the right-hand end of the axle in vise and removing left-hand nut and washers. Then you remove the left-hand cone and brake arm.

It will be found that the left-hand ball cup does not have a seperate dust cap and that the balls are not loose as they are held in a retainer.

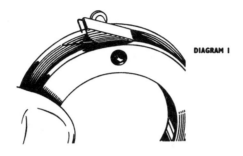

DIAGRAM I

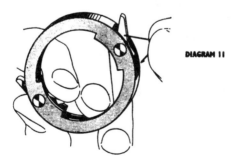

DIAGRAM II

Turn the hub over and unscrew the right-hand ball cup. As with the A.W., slide the assembly out of shell as one unit.

Clamp the axle assembly in vise by the cog side flats. Remove brake band, brake thrust plate and the planet cage pawl ring.

Reverse the axle assembly so that we are now holding the left hand end of the axle in the vise. We can now remove the driver right-hand ball cup. (Note that this still has loose balls and push fit dust cap).

Remove the gear ring pawl ring and gear ring from assembly.

Next take off the clutch assembly, cap, spring thrust ring and washer (if in two parts) axle key, clutch and clutch sleeve.

This leaves the planet cage and planets. Pull out the pins and planets.

Remove the axle from vise, turn it over and carefully remove the "C" shaped circlip at the base of the planet cage adjacent to the threads. Now remove the planet cage.

Before assembling you will naturally check all parts for wear and you will replace any worn bearing parts, as in driver and right-hand ball cup.

Replace weak pawl springs and worn pawls as per previous T.C.W. old-type hub instructions.

Some other things for you to check are the following:

Make sure that the "C" circlip fits snug and tight in its canalure on the axle.

See that the brake actuating spring has a good tension and that the ends are not worn. Likewise, the clutch and all engaging surfaces, such as dogs on gear ring and the tops of pinion pins.

Once you have made sure all of your bearing surfaces and retainers are well greased you can now proceed to assemble.

First, slide planet cage on axle and secure with "C" circlip.

Now, grip axle, left-hand end by the flats in the vise with slot uppermost.

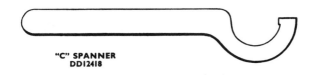

"C" SPANNER
DD12418

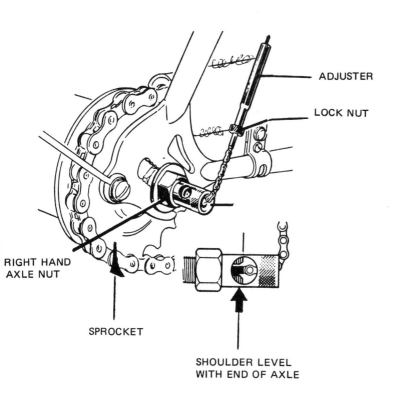

ADJUSTER

LOCK NUT

RIGHT HAND
AXLE NUT

SPROCKET

SHOULDER LEVEL
WITH END OF AXLE

ADJUSTING   STURMEY ARCHER
3-SPEED

Next, install the pinions with their pins, making sure that the flats are pointing downwards.

Now, install the clutch assembly and the remainder of the three-speed part of the hub. The same way as for the T.C.W. old style hub which we have previously described.

Having finished this side to the point where we have tightened up the right-hand lock-nut, reverse the axle set so that we now grip the right-hand end of the axle in the vise.

Install the planet cage pawl ring with the legs uppermost. Seat it correctly with the flats on the pinion pins facing out.

If we have to replace the actuating spring, make sure it seats over the legs of the pawl ring.

Rotate the pawl ring until the thrust ring seats against flat of the pawl ring assembly.

Now we can place the brake band in position with the keys facing upwards.

Remove assembly from vise and holding the right-hand ball cup in the right-hand, carefully guide assembly into the hub shell which you can hold in the left-hand.

Rotate the right-hand ball cup until you can hear the pawls click into place. Continue rotating until cup is threaded up against the hub shell.

With the drift punch and hammer lock it in place. If the dust cap was removed from the left-hand cone, likewise the brake arm, these can now be replaced.

Make sure that you align keyways on dust cap and cone before tapping lightly with a hammer to seat it.

Now you can seat the brake arm and this can also be tapped into place.

Put the axle, right-hand end again in the vise and install the ball retainer, correct way up!

Check to see the leg of spring is in between keys of the brass brake band before sliding brake arm assembly onto axle.

The slots of the left-hand cone must coincide with the keys of the brake band.

Now install brake arm lock-nut, small side first. Follow this with washer and outer locknut.

Screw brake arm nut down finger-tight and then back off slightly. Hold it in position with a "C" spanner, and then tighten down outer lock-nut.

You will find that with most of these hubs a very slight amount of play is acceptable.

If sprocket was removed, replace in the order it came off; this, of course, will also apply to the washers.

Most 3-speed hub and coaster 3-speeds have two lengths of axles and it is important to know that when this component has to be replaced, make sure the same length of both axle and indicator are used. Otherwise, difficulty in adjusting the gear could be experienced.

Hubs that have a single rod and chain on the right-hand side are adjusted as follows:

With the trigger or control in middle (normal and not neutral as some people seem to think) the first shoulder on the rod should be flush with the end of the axle. This can usually be seen through the window on the right-hand elongated nut.

It should be noted that with the MKIII hub gear ring, a K511A gear ring should never be substituted for the correct combination of K322 gear ring and K4852 gear ring pawl ring.

These numbers are Raleigh part numbers and will be found in their spare parts list, and likewise on their spare parts boxes.

Hubs that are in general usage should be lubricated every month with a good quality oil such as Raleigh oil or Schwinn bicycle oil.

Sprockets to fit Sturmey Archer 3-splined drivers are available as follows: 16th to 20th: 22nd is also available.

Apart from the handlebar trigger controls, there are also twist grip controls. At the time of this writing two examples are likely to be found.

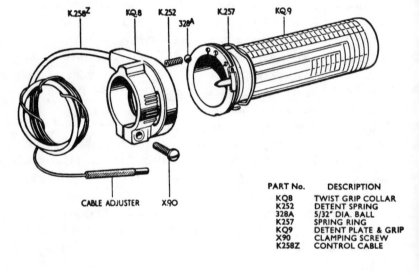

K.258Z   KQ8   K.252   328A   K.257   KQ9

CABLE ADJUSTER   X90

PART No.	DESCRIPTION
KQ8	TWIST GRIP COLLAR
K252	DETENT SPRING
328A	5/32″ DIA. BALL
K257	SPRING RING
KQ9	DETENT PLATE & GRIP
X90	CLAMPING SCREW
K258Z	CONTROL CABLE

First, let us look at the earlier pattern. It is held in place on the handlebar with a single screw.

In order to remove and dismantle, we must undo this screw and slide grip off from the handlebar.

Place cable end of twist grip on bench and with a screwdriver remove the spring from behind collar. Next, remove grip with detent plate from collar. Be careful that you do not lose the ball or spring.

If you have to fit a new cable, lay collar down on the bench. Fit nipple of new cable into the socket in grip detent plate and install wire into fluting around rim of detent plate.

Please note that sometimes the nipple needs a little grease to fit nicely into recess.

Place the detent spring into spring cavity with 5/32 ball on top. Use a small amount of grease.

Here are Raleigh's own words regarding the fitting of a cable:

"First fit detent spring and the 3/16" diameter ball into recess in operating sleeve and use grease to hold spring and ball in position.

"Fit cable nipple into slotted recess of opening sleeve.

"Fit cable inner wire into slot of gear locating spring and position this spring over operatating sleeve.

"Check that the 3/16" ball is positioned in elongated hole of gear locating spring.

"Keeping thumb of right hand over the ball and spring feed inner wire into cable slot of bottom half of casing.

"Now press locating spring into casing—until spring clicks *right down* into its groove.

"Fit top half of casing over operating sleeve and holding two halves of casing together, fit clamping screws.

"Refit twist-grip on the handlebar and take up any slackness in control cable. Adjust gears at hub end."

HSJ 583 Twist Grip complete with Cable and Spare Grip

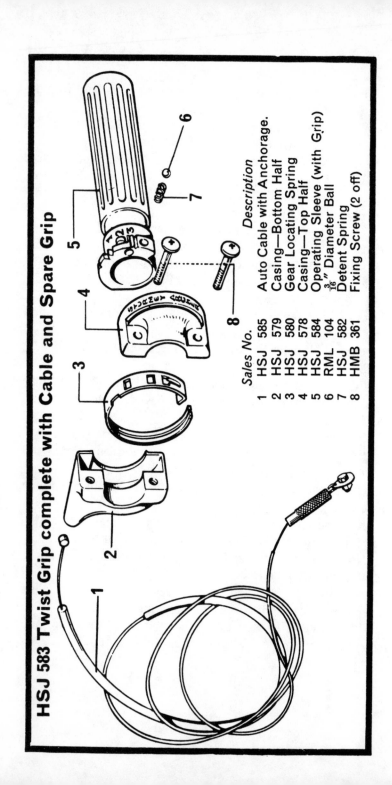

Sales No.		Description
1	HSJ 585	Auto Cable with Anchorage.
2	HSJ 579	Casing—Bottom Half
3	HSJ 580	Gear Locating Spring
4	HSJ 578	Casing—Top Half
5	HSJ 584	Operating Sleeve (with Grip)
6	RML 104	$\frac{3}{16}$" Diameter Ball
7	HSJ 582	Detent Spring
8	HMB 361	Fixing Screw (2 off)

S.3.C. THREE SPEED COASTER HUB

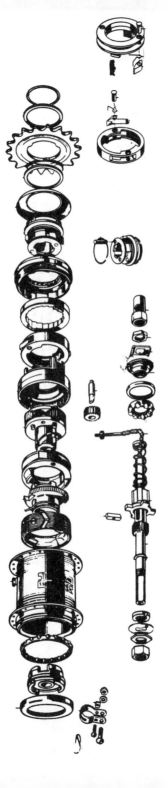

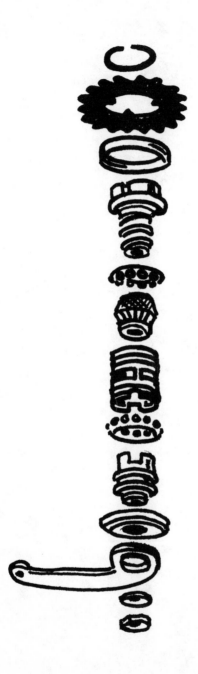

KOMET

9

HANDLEBARS, GOOSENECKS AND TAPING

We have discussed goosenecks briefly in the chapter on fork removal. They are known by various names, such as handlebar stems or extensions, and in the United States they are called "goosenecks".

It is interesting to note that in Great Britain a certain type of curved stem is known as a "swan neck".

Today they are mostly held in place with a device known as an "expander bolt".

This is a long bolt which passes through the entire length of the gooseneck; the top is furnished with a hex head, while the bottom end that is threaded, engages a wedge.

In the European type the wedge is in the shape of a truncated cone which is pulled up into the slotted end of the stem; this expands it to grip the inside of the fork column, when the bolt is tightened.

Most American models favor the sloping top type of wedge, this corresponds to the sloping angle of the bottom of the gooseneck.

On better quality goosenecks you will find that the hex head of the expander is being replaced by an Allen socket which is usually flush with the top and presents a cleaner look.

We have talked earlier on removal of goosenecks but we will recap a little for you now.

Undo the top nut two or three turns until it sticks up approximately 1/4 of an inch, and then with a copper mallet tap it down.

This will free the wedge from the bottom of the stem and enable you to withdraw the handlebars and gooseneck.

It is important to remember when replacing to make sure you have at least 2 1/2 inches of the stem in the fork column—so much so that several manufacturers put a maximum height mark on the metal.

Do not overtighten the expander.

If the bicycle falls over and hits the handlebar—the latter should turn. Overtightening simply puts a "pucker" or bulge in the fork column.

Just tighten sufficiently so that when the bicycle is ridden the handlebars and fork will stay in line with each other.

Another thing you should check when installing a new gooseneck is that you have the correct diameter.

For many years stems were 7/8" but with the present popularity of people raising up handlebars, particularly of the High Rise Sting-Ray variety, a spate of fork column breakages occurred.

So many, in fact, that several manufacturers have increased the thickness of the column which necessitated using a smaller diameter gooseneck—13/16" to be precise.

If you have a fork that is made for 7/8" stem and can only obtain the 13/16" type, use the special adapter which should come with the gooseneck.

This will be in the form of a flanged ferrule or outside sleeve, which increases the outer diameter of the stem; the flange prevents it from sliding down too far into the column.

We have been speaking of the stem part of the gooseneck.

Now we come to the part that holds the handlebar, this can be in some cases integral with the handlebars.

This will be found mostly in the upright comfort raised type of bar; the drawback to this kind of arrangement is, of course, that the rider can not tilt the bar to his or her own riding position.

On the adjustable type, the handlebar is held in place with a nut and bolt, sometimes just a bolt, the neck of the stem itself is threaded to receive it.

This is known in the United States as the "Binder Bolt", and when in the nut and bolt form it is often interchangeable with the frame seat bolt.

It is usually fitted with a locking pip under the head which fits into a slot coming away from the hole in the gooseneck.

Very often when tightening, this will round off, in which instance I would suggest removing and replacing with a suitable size hex head nut and bolt.

You can then hold the head with a wrench while tightening the nut. If you ever have a real tough bolt that refuses to tighten or loosen even with the head held by the "vise grip", the best solution that I have found is to hold the hacksaw horizontally and saw the bolt in half in between the upper and lower part of the gooseneck extension.

This extension piece will be found close up or really extended sometimes as much as 5" depending on the driver's reach. (See later notes on "Major Taylor").

When renewing handlebars care must be taken to get the right size middle part.

Most steel handlebars are 7/8" with a raised portion in the center.

American handlebars are normally thicker in the center than their European counterparts.

So do not expect a Raleigh made handlebar to fit into an American-made gooseneck without using a sleeve or ferrule.

I always save old pumps, both the steel and aluminum kinds, they make excellent sleeves —cut them to the correct width of the gooseneck and then slice them.

The angle of the extension piece varies; from upward tilting to downward, you will find curving in both pieces.

At least two famous bicycle riders have given their names to goosenecks.

The first was the great American-Negro rider who was known as Major Taylor and was a champion in the 1890's.

He originated and used a gooseneck which consisted of stem and extension. The extension was of a diamond form and had a sliding handlebar clamp mounted on it, permitting

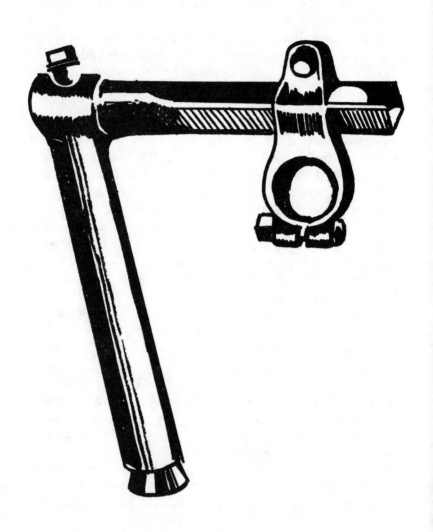

MAJOR TAYLOR ADJUSTABLE GOOSENECK

HANDLEBARS
GOOSENECKS

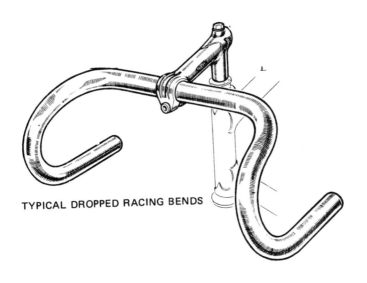

TYPICAL DROPPED RACING BENDS

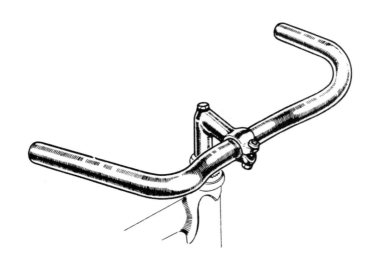

COMFORT BARS

SEAT PILLARS AND SEAT CLIPS

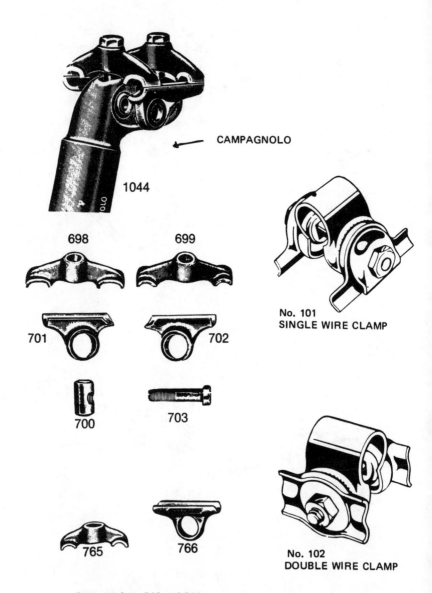

CAMPAGNOLO

1044

698

699

701

702

700

703

765

766

No. 101
SINGLE WIRE CLAMP

No. 102
DOUBLE WIRE CLAMP

Part numbers 765 and 766
may be used to make
1045 Seat Post

830   1071

the rider to adjust his forward position.

Judging by the photos we have seen of Taylor, he had the handlebars on top of the extension in contrast with the way they are used today, the bars are usually slung underneath.

The other famous rider that is remembered by his handlebar stem is the German Toni Merkens, he used the track gooseneck which curved down and forward until it reached nearly half-way down the head tube.

Steel handlebars as we have stated come normally in 7/8" width, but 15/16" and 1 inch have been found. This follows also with the aluminum alloy patterns.

Most of the dropped racing handlebars are either named after great riders, places or types of races.

Thus we have Maes, Binda, Marsh, Lauterwasser and Bailey to name just a few who perpetuate the memory of famous riders.

The names of North Road, South of France, Shallow Highgate bring to mind three places that are actively associated with bicycling activities.

Some shapes over the years have changed their names. The B.S.A. Continental that was popular when I was in my early twenties is now known as the Le Randonneur.

Most 3-speed or coaster lightweight type bicycles use either an inverted North Road or a Raleigh Comfort Raised bar.

These are O.K. for short distances, but for long trips dropped handlebars with their 3 different positions are the best.

In Britain and Europe a shape that has long been popular seems now to becoming very popular in the United States. This is the Anelay or Allrounder. The Peugeot Ladies twin-top tube bicycle fits these as standard and they are a comfortable "bend".

In their shape they resemble the type of handlebar which has been used for years on motor cycles.

"Dropped handlebars" sometimes get bent as the result of

a collision or a fall.

Unless they are really bad, these can generally be straightened by laying the bicycle on its side and resting the foot on the grounded part of the bars, and finally by exerting upward pressure with both hands on the other end.

Care has to be taken to keep not only the angle of the bars similar but to keep the drops parallel.

It is important that the ends of all handlebars are kept plugged or masked in one way or another.

Raised bars are generally fitted with grips. These can be a problem at times to remove.

If new ones are to be fitted we do not have to worry. Simply cut the old ones off.

But if they are to be used again we can not do this—here are some tips:

First of all take a crescent wrench and close the jaws until they nearly grip the bars.

Now push with a twisting motion up against the grip that you wish to remove—I find this method rarely fails unless the grips are stuck on.

Here I will usually stick a very thin screwdriver or spoke down under the grip, raise up slightly, and then squirt some W.D. 40 down; grasp the grip with a piece of cloth and give it a forceful twist.

After doing this a few times, you should be able to remove it.

Care must be taken when you have it off; clean and dry out the inside thoroughly, otherwise, it will be inclined not to stay on when replaced.

The other practical tip requires a colleague to help you.

Get him to seal up one end while you put the air hose with the blower attachment to the other.

As you let go with the air give your grip a twist—again, this will generally do the trick.

Dropped bars are usually taped and plugged. The plugs are either spring steel or rubber with a thread insertion part, or made of plastic with an expander nut and bolt through the middle.

In order to remove, insert a screwdriver tip under the flange and pry out if one of the first two patterns.

If it is the expander type simply undo the screw with a driver and then pull out the plug.

You will find the tape is just wrapped around. To remove start at the plug end and unwind.

Sometimes you will find that adhesive tape has been used, in which case, I get a sharp knife, and following the contour of the bars make a cut from one end of the tape to the other (that is at right angles to the wrappings).

Now you will find, with a bit of luck, that you can peel the whole lot off in one go.

I do not like sticky tape. If you have hot hands or the day happens to be warm, after riding for a short time, the stuff tends to ooze out and makes everything sticky.

My preference when it is obtainable is for twill cloth tape; otherwise plastic tape that is not sticky is the solution.

If the tape comes in one reel, it is a good idea to unroll it and divide into two halves.

The British-made Gem tape comes in two reels so we do not have to worry about doing this.

Start about two or three inches from the gooseneck, (again, this is my personal choice) place the end under the bar and keeping your finger on it until the last minute, start to wrap the tape overlapping the end completely and pull tight.

If you can not do this, secure the end with a little scotch tape.

Now continue to wrap, overlapping each turn half way and keep it tight.

When you come to the brake levers, diagonally cross the housing top and bottom; if you are not used to it, keep checking under the bar so that you do not leave any gaps.

Continue wrapping until we come to the end of the bar.

Overlap the bar about half way and tuck the remainder inside, then follow up and finish with the plug—if of the expander type, tighten up the screw.

If you are fitting any rubber brake hoods or lever coverings, do this before taping—but do not attempt to put these on dry.

This goes for grips too—you will find that you will get the fitting on half-way and then it sticks or splits.

Soapy water is the answer, you should never use oil.

Going back to the tape, you will find it easier to wrap the bars with the tape rolled up, similar to a nurse putting on a bandage.

If you unrolled it to divide into two, re-roll it before taping your bars.

If you have safety levers on your brakes, it is a good "wheeze" to remove these while taping.

Before leaving the subject, do not forget, if you have finger tip controls for your gears, tape the outer casing to the bars.

In this case the plug end of the controls take the play off the normal end plugs.

Carefully remove the pivot bolts, laying them out in sequence, most plugs of this kind require an Allen key wrench to tighten or loosen.

This controls a form of an expander plug and must be kept tight as quite a little pressure is put on the controls when gear shifting.

When taping these cables be careful to allow enough sweep to permit normal turning of the handlebars.

HOW TO TAPE HANDLEBARS

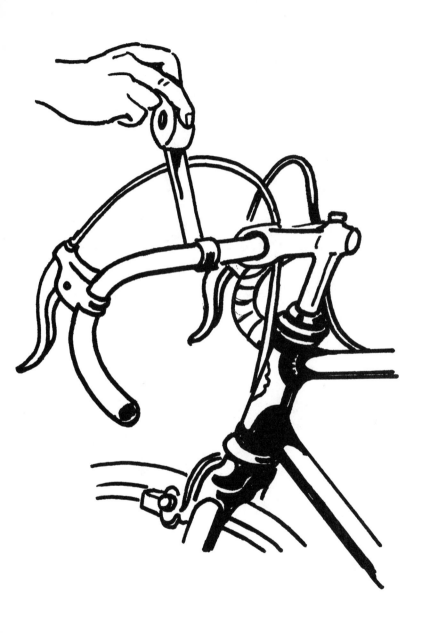

HOW TO WRAP THE TAPE AROUND THE BRAKE LEVER

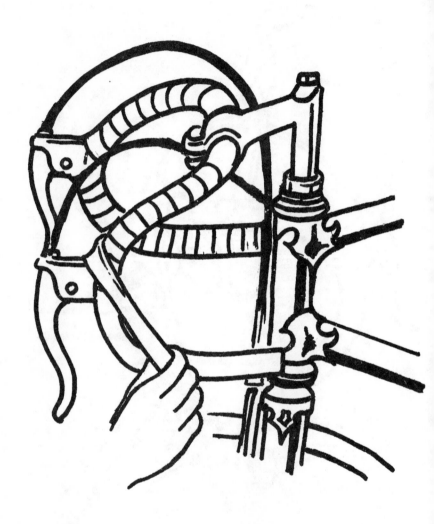

STEEL HANDLEBAR PLUG

PLASTIC HANDLEBAR PLUG

HANDLE BAR TAPE

RUBBER PLUG WITH SCREW EXPANDER

10

SEATS AND PILLARS

The seat pillar stem, post, or whatever you wish to call it, is that piece of tubing that fits into the frame and supports the seat or saddle.

It is made of steel or aluminum alloy, today it is generally straight; in the old days, it was often "L" Shaped, the idea was to give the bicyclist more lateral adjustment in his riding position.

We must be careful when renewing this component to install a longer post as they will come in a large number of diameters.

At one end of the scale we have the thin Schwinn post which fits their 1 inch diameter bicycle frame up to seat posts of approximately 1 1/16 inch diameter made for 1 1/8 frame tubes.

Even frames with the same outside diameter seat tubes can take several different sizes of posts; this is due to the different gauges of frame tubing used.

In some cases it is possible to use a smaller post utilizing a sleeve somewhat after the style of the gooseneck ferrule.

If we do not have one, here is a tip that can often get you out of difficulty.

By using the small cap from a Schwinn spray can we can make a sleeve; with a pair of twin tin snips carefully cut the top off.

Now reduce the size by cutting a piece out of the side, and by careful tapping we can form it around our post until it fits snugly. If the ends meet cut off another piece.

The lip on our erstwhile cap acts like the flange on the handlebar ferrule and stops it from slipping down into the seat tube of the frame, always put the cut out part, adjacent to the slot, on the seat clamp.

If we are lucky and get the right size post to work with our made up sleeve, you will find that it does the job very well and does not look unsightly.

Some Peugeot bicycles came with undersized seat pillars a short time ago, and we were at our wits end to rectify this.

With sliding calipers I measured the diameter of some Sting-Ray handlebars and found them just a little larger.

Using some of these bars, we cut off the longest straight parts and found they made admirable substitute seat posts.

I merely mention this to show what can be done if you use a little ingenuity when you are working on your bicycle.

Most seats fit on the post with a clamp and serrated washers with a horizontally fitted bolt completing the arrangement.

It is important to keep this bolt very tight; if allowed to loosen, the two washers start to pivot and wear-off the serrations and then we can never tighten them without replacing the washers.

To assist us when installing seats, most manufacturers fit the larger clip, but supply the thick sleeve so that the seat can be used on either the thick European seat post or the thin American type.

Most seat posts are held in position by the bolt that is situated at the seat cluster lug but there are exceptions.

Some Japanese seat posts are made after the fashion of the gooseneck, that is, they use the expander bolt method of tightening.

This is not exactly the best of ideas—for one thing it is not always easy to get a wrench inside to get at the hex head of the expander bolt when the seat is installed.

Here is another thing to be considered; unless the frame tubing is of a fairly thick gauge, over tightening of the expander could easily put a bulge in it.

Another type of seat post that has been gaining in

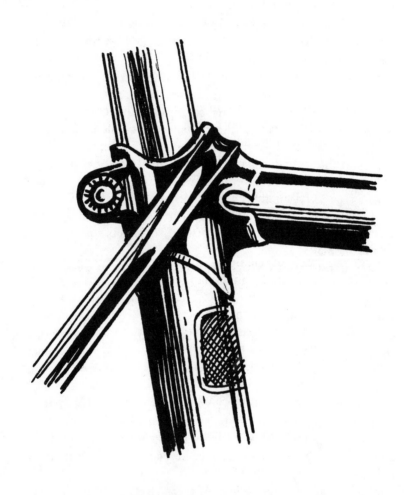

EXAMPLE OF SEAT CLUSTER

WITH WRAP-ROUND SEAT STAYS

popularity recently is the Campagnolo type. This does away with the conventional seat clamp and has instead a cradle fitted to the top of the seat post to which is further attached a set of brackets.

Two vertical bolts in brackets clamp across the wire framework of the seat onto two side supports and give a secure mounting.

This Campagnolo seat clamp comes in two sizes, one for wide cradle saddles with short adjustment, and the other for narrow cradles with long adjustment.

Returning to the frame seat post bolt, in most cases this is almost the same as the gooseneck binder bolt, (In many instances it is interchangeable) and the same problem can arise; that is, the pip or key under the head of the bolt can shear-off, so you should adopt the same remedy as for the gooseneck bolt.

Other methods of clamping include quick-release levers (these are used mainly in collapsible bicycles) and Allen sockets.

Sometimes you mechanics will encounter a customer's bicycle where the rider has rammed an oversize post into the frame. Here are a few tips to help you remove it.

With the seat removed, cut the smallest amount from the top of the post. This will be to remove the inside lip.

Now find a solid round piece of steel that will fit inside the post.

Now we can grip the top of the post with our "vise grip" without crushing it.

Take out the seat bolt and gently pry open the two parts of the seat lug and run some penetrating oil down between the post and the inside of the seat tube.

With someone holding the bicycle try a twisting motion with the vise grip—this will generally do the trick—and you should find you can unscrew the post out.

I have had some stubborn cases, and in extreme circumstances this is how I have solved the problem.

With the saddle removed I bronze welded a piece of tubing across the top of the post to form a letter "T".

The heat of the welding running down the post plus the increased leverage that is obtained by the horizontal tube— well, all I can say is that it has not failed me yet!

11

TIRES, INSTALLATION AND REPAIRS

We have already discussed tire and rim sizes in the chapter on wheels—Now how about tire and tube installation?

Let us assume that we put a bicycle up onto the rack to put a tire and tube on the rear wheel.

To do this I like to turn the bicycle upside down—but if you prefer to work with the machine the right side up, do so!

If the bicycle is derailleur equipped, make sure the rear gear lever is forward so that the chain is on the small cog of the cluster (freewheel).

Undo the rear nuts and pull the gear to the rear and then give the wheel a good tap forward, this should send it out of the dropouts.

To remove the tire, make sure that all the air is out of the tube; clip a valve key on the valve and press the tire all the way around.

This will also break any adhesion, if the tire has been on the rim.

Under certain climatic conditions tires will stick.

Push the valve into the tire about half of its length, at the same time pinch the tire at this area and push it towards the well of the rim. With the valve towards you, rest the axle of the hub up against the bench.

Now slide each hand around the tire going away from the valve. Compressing the tire into the well, you should be able to lift one side of the tire off the rim by about the time your hands are ready to meet.

You will notice I do not mention using levers or irons. These should be used only as a last resort for a really tough tire.

Practice the above directions, persevere and once you do acquire the knack you will wonder why you ever used levers. It also looks so much more professional to your customers.

Once you remove the tire and tube—do the job properly and whip off the rim strip. Inspect the spoke heads in the nipple.

If in any doubt set your narrow grindstone in motion and run the wheel around against the stone smoothing down any rough spots or protruding spoke ends.

Check the rim strip and if in any doubt replace it.

Taking your new tire, make sure it and the inner tube are the correct size.

Put a little air in the tube and fit it inside the tire. Thread the valve through the rim strip and rim valve hole; if necessary, lift the rim strip until the valve has completely penetrated the rubber.

Next, starting from the valve, put one side of the tire on, finishing at the point directly opposite the valve.

Come back to the valve and do the same thing to the other side. This time use the same technique as for taking off the tire.

If you get to the point where you have about 3 inches of the tire to get on and it is very hard—go back to the valve, push it in and jam your axle up against the bench.

Work your fingers around the tire again and you should be able to slip the tire over.

Sometimes you may find that you have too much air in the tube. Let a little out—but not all, otherwise you will pinch the tube under the bead of the tire.

If you just can not get that last part over, that is, sometimes in a thorn resistant tube (these tubes are about 3 times as thick as the normal tube) it makes it really tough to fit the tire.

Hold the wheel upright, the unfitted part at the bottom and towards you.

Now place this portion in the vise, the rim resting on the

top of the jaws. Close up the vise fairly tight.

Put your left hand approximately at 9 o'clock and your right hand at about 3 o'clock and with a swift twist to the rear of the vise you will find the tire will pop right on.

One thing that is important to remember. NEVER use tire levers or worst yet screwdrivers to put a tire on. It is almost impossible to do this without ripping the tube!

Next put a little more air in the tube and go around the tire making sure it is seating correctly.

Check the bead and try to get it as parallel as is possible to the rim.

Gradually increase the pressure until you have the right amount. In this case, a 27" x 1 1/4" tire requires, approximately 70 pounds.

If you find one part of the tire is stuck in the well of the rim and will not come up, deflate the tire and smear the area with soapy water—this acts as a lubricant and should allow the tire to slide up into position when next you inflate it.

Spin the wheel and check again.

Before you install the dust cap, put some of the soapy water in the valve—if it bubbles, try tightening the core—with your valve tool.

Some dust caps incorporate a keyed metal cap which can be used as such.

To replace the wheel slip the chain on the small cog—pull the gear back and slip the wheel into the dropouts—I should mention that if the brake is fitted with a quick-release this must be undone before taking out the wheel.

Tighten up the nuts, making sure the wheel is central in the frame.

It is best to push the wheel into the dropouts as far as it will go—if the gear is clamped to the frame, this will take care of the light side—if of the hanger variety the wheel stops should have been set previously and this will arrest the hub axle.

Tighten the right side first, this will allow you to play

around with the left side—check points of chainstay bridge and seatstay bridge.

If a quick-release axle, make sure you get a good bite when setting the lever. If too loose hold the lever with one hand and screw up the outer cone shaped nut with the other—now try the lever again.

If you are merely replacing the tube or patching same, be sure to check the tread of the tire for thorns, glass, tacks, etc.

If thorns are suspected, run around the inside of the tire with a piece of sandpaper.

Putting a patch on a tube today from the bicycle shop owner's point of view is not profitable for him.

It does not pay for him to patch inner tubes. Time is the great factor to be considered, particularly when he is trying to find a high pressure leak. The hole might be so small that when the tube is out of the tire he can not put enough air pressure in for the hole to open sufficiently to show; even when immersed in water.

Another drawback is even when he finds and patches the hole—he can not guarantee that there are not any more smaller holes. However, be that as it may, let us assume that we have to patch a tube.

The first thing, of course, would be to find the hole.

If it is large, all we have to do is put air into the tube and see or feel where it comes out.

Mark the spot with an indelible pencil.

Next, clean the spot thoroughly with fine sandpaper overlapping the space that is needed for a patch.

Now, we put a thin film of cement over the cleaned part.

Allow to almost dry and then after peeling off the protecting calico from the patch, press down firmly over the hole.

The final step is to stitch down the hole with a roller stick if you have one; if you do not have such a stick use the handle of a knife.

Make sure that the patch is large enough to cover the hole;

it should overlap about a 1/4 inch all around.

If the hole or gash in the tire is so big that the tube pokes through—a temporary measure would be to put a boot inside.

It pays for you to keep on hand an old tubular or sew-up tire. From this you can make excellent boots because of the fact that it will have such a thin thread. When cut and laid flat it does not make too much of a bulge inside the tire.

We have spoken about patching normal tubes with cold patches. How about the thick thorn resisting types? Cold patches normally do not work too well on these tubes. The answer is a hot patch.

We prepare the tube as for an ordinary patch, but this time we use the hot variety.

This consists of a metal tray on the bottom of which is a piece of rubber; these come in round and oval shapes, and inside the tray is a combustible material.

We peel off the protective coating from the patch and place it over the hole. We then have to clamp it down.

If we do not have the correct appliance, we can use a "C" clamp with a couple of pieces of thin metal, a wide piece for under the tube and a narrow piece to rest across the tray.

With a spoke or something similar, dig into the stuff inside the tray, this will make it easier to light.

Make sure that all the material burns and then leave it for 5 minutes.

When this time has elapsed undo the clamp and remove the tray—you will find the patch nicely vulcanized.

By way of interest, you can also use the hot patch on ordinary tubes following exactly the same procedure.

To do the job correctly, you should dust all patches, etc. with talc before replacing it in the tire.

Returning to boots for a moment, you will find that with careful positioning no adhesive is really necessary. The pressure of the tube will hold the boot in place.

With a new tube always check the valve core with water or use your two pronged valve tool to see whether or not the core insert is loose.

Be careful when doing this as the cores are somewhat delicate—make sure that you locate the flats on the insert before tightening. Most tubes in the United States use Schrader valves.

In some high pressure tubes and of course in "sew-ups" you will find the "Presta" type valve.

When using this type be careful to keep the little "bobble" on top screwed down when passing it through the valve hole in rim strip or actual rim. This little "bobble" comes into view when the dust cap is removed.

To inflate the tube or tire unscrew the "bobble" all the way. Screw on your pump connection or hose and pump up in the normal way.

If you are using the air hose and compressor you will need a small brass adapter which screws over the "Presta" converting it into almost a Schrader valve.

If it is hard to get air into the tube, experiment with the "bobble" and try screwing it back a little way.

Another type of valve that you may come across is the "Woods" valve.

This consists of a valve barrel about the size of a "Schrader", but has no screwed in core; instead there are two slots cut vertically in the top, an equal distance from each other.

These locate the two protruding bars on the shouldered pin which fits inside the valve barrel.

The lower portion of this pin is tapered and takes a thin sleeve of rubber.

The pin is drilled from the top, the hole emerging on the side of the taper, where it is covered by the valve rubber.

When air is pumped in, the rubber expands, allowing air to go into the tube, but contracts to keep the air in the moment that pumping stops.

The pin is held in place by a cap which screws on the top of the valve barrel. The top of the pin is also threaded and takes a dust cap. Some years ago, the "Aligaro" pin was introduced to do away with the valve rubbered pin; this only becomes apparent when it is withdrawn as the top is identical.

The tapered part is of the spring and washer type and is something like a Schrader valve core.

Valves always used to be bolted into the tube and if you come across this kind always check the hex nut base.

Today most valves are vulcanized to the tube but you should still check the junction at the base.

People do not keep their tire pressure up and riding on soft tires results in several bad things. Apart from rim cuts and bruises, the valve stems cockle and result in cuts at the base.

We will now discuss tubular tires and sew-ups.

Although lightweight high pressure wired on tires can be made light and responsive when mounted on light aluminum rims, the ultimate demanded by bicycle racers are the tubular tires that are installed on their special rims.

They are variously called "Sprints & Tubs", "Sew-ups", "Singles", and come in a variety of different weights.

"Clement", a famous manufacturer of such tires, lists a very light tire known as Criterium Silk which weighs 6.60 ounces.

On the other hand "Clement" has the "Elvezici" which is cotton vulcanized and weighs 15.80 ounces. There are many other weights listed in between the aforementioned two tires.

Other famous makers of tubulars include "D'Alessandro", "Constrictor", "Pirelli", and "Dunlop".

The tubular tire consists of a very thin casing wrapped around an exceedingly thin inner tube.

Where the casing meets it is sewn, thus the tire and tube are one, hence the Australian term "Singles" or as they are know in America, "Sew-ups". As there are no wire beads or lips on the rim, the tires have to be glued or cemented on the rims.

"Vittoria" super-white cement is a very fine example of cement that can be used for either track or road racing needs.

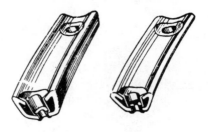

Rims for tubular tires (sew-ups)
showing ferruled spoke holes.

No. 700S SPORTS

Rims for tubular tires (sew-ups)
showing washers

No. 700M MONTLHERY

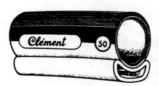

Typical tubular tire mounted on
sprint rim.

No. 19: Clément
50 semi-professional

Example of wired on tire mounted on Westwood rim.

Example of steel tubular on
Lightweight rim.

Example of steel tubular Lightweight rim with serrated side
walls.

Other choices include "Clement" cement and, "Mastice Gutta" which is recommended for road work.

Double sided sticky tape is preferred by some instead of cement.

As we have stated so many times before in this manual you will find arguments for and against when dealing with any specialized equipment.

A lot depends, to a certain extent, on the rider and his own preferences.

Be that as it may, we are more concerned here with repair and installation so let us see how we would go about installing a tubular tire.

First of all, make sure that all spoke heads and nipples are below the tire seating surface of the rim.

Anything sticking up could either pierce the tire or at best damage the stitching.

Assuming in this case that we are going to attach the tire to the rim with cement—spread some all around the rim seating.

The cement comes either in a tube or container with a brush—the latter makes it easier to apply.

Whatever method you use, try to get it even. Two or three thin coats are better than one thick lumpy coat.

Referring to our previous remarks about personal preference, some riders use shellac which gives an excellent adhesion. The only drawback to this method is that it makes for harder quick tire changing.

But returning to the normal cement—allow it to get tacky.

Next, insert valve through valve hole remembering what we said about the "bobble" on the top of the valve stem.

Now rest the hub axle up against the bench, the wheel in a horizontal position.

Starting from each side of the valve, grip the tire and pushing it away from you, gently stretch the tire onto the rim.

It is important to try and keep each side equal so as to

keep the valve upright.

Partially inflate the tire and go all around making sure it is seated correctly. That is, the sidewalls are parallel to the rim on each side.

Now build up the pressure—here again the rider's choice, weight, etc., is generally the deciding factor.

As a general guide, most tire makers suggest the following: For smooth tracks, rear tires 90 to 120 lbs. For road racing, approximately 80 to 100 lbs. Front tires usually about 10 lbs. less than the rear. Most manufacturers recommend allowing some time to elapse before using the bicycle.

Some even go so far as to suggest waiting 24 hours for maximum adhesion.

Repairing tubulars is something most bicycle repair shops balk at. In these times of high labor costs, it just does not pay for them to do so.

Most riders, therefore, must learn to do their own "sew-up" repairs.

We will run through a normal patching operation for those who are interested.

Make sure all the air is out of the tire and remove from the rim.

Now inflate and check to see where the air is coming out. If necessary immerse in water.

Having found the puncture, mark the position.

Now carefully detach the rim tape about 3 to 4 inches each side of the leakage.

Before cutting the stitching, put a few marks across at intervals.

This will insure when we restitch that we will get the two sides equal and can use the exact opposite stitching holes, and will insure that the tire keeps its shape and does not cockle up.

With a razor blade or other sharp knife carefully cut the stitching, this will expose the inside protecting tape.

Pull this to one side and gently pull out the section of the tube to be patched.

Clean the tube carefully with a very fine sandpaper and wipe off the dust with a clean rag.

Put a thin film of cement on the area surrounding the hole, let it get tacky (almost dry) and remove the backing from the patch.

Use the special thin patches for such tubes as Romac Cure-C.; press on firmly and knead it down.

Sprinkle talc over the patch and surrounding area. This will prevent the tube from sticking to the tire.

Examine the casing and should there be a fracture in the fabric put a piece of patching canvas on the inside of the tire.

Make sure there is no foreign matter inside the casing before replacing the tube.

Insure that the inside tape is correctly positioned before you start stitching.

Hold the tire between the fingers so that the tube is out of the way and the marks that we made are opposite each other.

Now carefully restitch the casing.

When we get to the last part, it is a good idea to use a blunt object.

The end of a pencil is ideal to poke down, to insure that the tube is not in the way of the needle as we complete the sewing.

Finally, flatten out the casing and cement the rim tape in position over the stitching.

Your tire is now ready to refit on the rim in the normal manner.

12

TOOLS AND TERMS

(TOOLS)

In order to do good work it is essential, not only to posess the "know how", but to have the right tools and a place in which to put that knowledge to good usage.

BENCH   A good bench is one of the first considerations. It should be strong and rugged enough to withstand plenty of wrenching, pulling and hammering. Height is another important factor – if anything, it is better to be too high rather than being too low – the mechanic can always stand on duckboards.

VISE   Next on your list of essentials is a good strong vise. Again, this should be mounted securely and at the correct height. The usual height is about 3' 6" to the top of the jaws, but this will obviously vary with the user.

CLAMPS   For light or medium work, it is necessary to use clamps to prevent the work from being damaged. These clamps are often made of lead, zinc, brass or other soft sheet metal. Lead clamps may not give you the best service, since lead when squeezed out of shape has to be recast for further use.

HACKSAW   When using a vise, decide first which will be the best method of holding the job. Avoid crushing the work or marking it unnecessarily. If you use a hacksaw, see that the saw-cut is placed as near to the jaws as is possible. Do not let the saw or file come into contact with the hardened jaws. This will spoil the tool rather than injuring the jaws.

Keep the vise clean by using a brush. If oil is left on the body, the filings will stick to the oil making it difficult to keep the vise clean. Occasionally oil the thread and nut, etc. Do not use the vise as an anvil, except for light work.

Stiffness and rigidity of the frame are essential, but at the same time the frame must not be clumsy. A modern development of the hacksaw is the tubular frame with the pistol grip. In order to saw a long piece down the side of a plate, the saw blade is turned at right angles to the frame.

The blade should be tightened up so that it "twangs" when plucked by the thumb. Also see that is true and parallel, before starting to saw with the teeth pointing forward to cut on that stroke. When cutting soft mild steel or cast iron, you should use a coarse blade, 14 teeth per inch. For cutting plate such as small bars, brass, etc., a medium blade of 22 or 24 teeth is used.

The finer toothed blade of 32 per inch must be used on tubes such as frame tubing, thin plates and cast steel. It should be understood that the above is only a general recommendation. In order to do good sawing the mechanic should stand squarely in front of the vise with the left foot forward similar to the position for filing. Do not get on top of the work, but stand some distance back.

Get the saw carefully lined up for the cut and start sawing. Downward pressure is put on the forward stroke, the pressure being released, so that the saw slides back barely in contact with the material on the backward stroke.

The whole motion should be rythmical and not in a series of jerks. Fifty strokes a minute is generally accepted as the correct speed.

FILES   There are three main grades of cut. Bastard, second cut and smooth files. The rough and bastard files are mostly used for heavy cutting. Most normal work is performed by the second cut. The smooth (and sometimes dead-smooth) files are used for finishing. Shape is also important – this of course will depend on the nature of the work involved.

Here are some of the different types of files:

(1) Hand file – generally has one edge uncut or "safe"

and is parallel in its width. Used for filing cotter pins and the collar on the fork crown.

(2) Pillar file — is somewhat like the hand but is narrower in width. Used for removing burrs, etc. from rear dropout slots.

(3) Half-round file — is self-explanatory.

(4) Round, rat-tail, square, triangular and warding filing. Used for frame lug

The "Modus operandi" should follow the technique of hacksawing and constant practice is necessary before one of the hardest of operations that befall the mechanic can be accomplished with skill. Always make sure that the handle is fitted securely on the tang together with a ferrule which will prevent the wood from splitting.

HAMMERS The ball-peen hammer is the type most used in any form of engineering, and one with the head about 3/4 pound will be found the most useful. Smaller heads are handy for riveting. A cross-peen or Warrington hammer should be among the tools of a bicycle mechanic.

Copper, lead and rawhide mallets or hammers will also prove their worth when it is necessary to use force without damaging the work.

CHISELS A good selection of chisels, drift punches and center punches is another must. Sometimes, the only way to remove an obstinant bolt is to resort to the chisel. When using these tools always be careful that you warn any people in the immediate vicinity, as flying chips can cause nasty wounds.

DRIFT PUNCHES Those of steel and brass or copper are most useful for removing stubborn notched lock rings and lock nuts. We should add here that a can of penetrating oil used in conjunction with the above should always be within easy reach.

CENTER PUNCHES Before drilling, the work should always be prepared with a "center pop" from the center punch. The point should ground to an angle of approximately 60 degrees. As with the chisels the pointed end should be hardened and tempered and the hammer end left soft.

SCREWDRIVERS A good seleltion of screwdrivers both for slotted heads and Phillips bolts should be kept in the bench rack. Thin bladed types are most useful both for derailleur gear adjustments and for prying out dust caps. It is a good plan to have some of the larger sizes fitted with hexagonal ferrules. This enables a wrench to be used when dealing with really stubborn bolts and screws.

Three sizes of Phillips type will be found useful. Phillips headed bolts are being found more and more on bicycle accessories, particularly on Japanese-made bicycles. Last in the range of screwdrivers but not the least is the Weinman Screwdriver for the Weinman brake-lever.

STEEL SQUARE and STEEL RULE These two tools will be used mostly by the bicycle mechanic in frame and fork repairs. Wherever possible they should be kept seperately from the other tools and handled with care.

SLIDING CALIPERS Here again is a tool which will be found handy in measuring distances in frame and fork straightening and tracking, also for checking gooseneck and seat pillar sizes.

TAPS AND DIES Some sizes will be found hard to obtain in these times of critical bicycle parts shortages, but whenever possible you should collect a good selection. Here are some of the essentials: Pedal taps, left and right, both 1/2" x 20" for American bicycles and 9/16" x 20" for European and most Japanese bicycles.

Bottom bracket taps, 1 3/8" x 26" T.P.I. at this time are very hard to get, but you should obtain them as soon as supplies are normal. Include on your list fork column dies 1" x 24" T.P.I., 1" x 25" T.P.I. and 1" x 26" T.P.I. In case T.P.I. is unfamiliar to you, it is short for threads per inch.

Also, the following axle dies sizes: (3/8" x 24"), (5/16" x 24"), (3/8" x 26"), and (5/16" x 26"), can often get you out of trouble should speed be essential when dealing with damaged axle threads and replacing the axle is not desired. Various other taps and dies from time to time will prove useful.

REAMERS You should have a selection of reamers on hand as they too will prove beneficial. They are used for enlarging holes, for installing larger bolts. In the case of 3 piece cranks — a tight fitting crank can be made a lot easier with the right size reamer run through the axle hole.

CRESCENT OR ADJUSTABLE WRENCHES A crescent wrench should be in every mechanic's tool kit. Some people may frown on the excessive use of adjustable wrenches, but today with the multitude of patterns, sizes, etc. of nuts found on bicycles, it is not always possible to have a correct wrench for every nut. In such cases the crescent is worth its weight in lime juice!

The eight inch will prove to be the most handy along with the six inch for smaller nuts, while the larger wrench is a must for such sizes as head nuts and bottom-bracket lock-nuts. Let us not forget the right-hand bottom-bracket cup. (See chapter on this part of the bicycle for instructions on how to make a useful gadget to use in conjunction with this tool).

POWER TOOLS A pistol type electric drill is another very handy tool, especially when the work is too large or awkward to fit under the drill press. (Apart from its use as a drill always keep a good range of well sharpened twist drills and do not forget to use always a Pilot before using the final size). The drill can be used with routers and small grinding bits for internal grinding. But we are digressing, let us return to wrenches.

You should include a couple of good pedal wrenches. These are long enough to give good leverage and thin enough to get in between the pedal crank. Next, we need a good selection of cone wrenches. "Var" makes a very good set of two 13-14 and 15-16. You will find that these will fit most front and rear hubs.

While the old "New Departure" cone and lock nut wrenches are ideal for this type of hub, we must not forget the Bendix range. Their cone and locknut spanner fit all of their single speed coaster hubs. While the locknut spanner will also fit the right-hand cone on the Bendix 2-speed hub range, a special two pronged tool is needed for the inserted locknut.

Speaking of cones, another very handy tool is the offset cone pliers. There are times when either the cone is not slotted or the use of a normal wrench is just not possible — hence the offset cone pliers.

WEINMAN SIX PIECE WRENCH SET, MAFAC SET AND THIRD HAND   These three tools for cable brakes is another must for the workshop. I have always been a tool magpie and have over the years collected all sorts of wrenches and tools and find that most of them are useful at one time or another. What I am saying here is that you can not have too many. To give you an example, I have one huge wrench—the only thing that it will fit is the right-hand stationary cone of the Schwinn hanger crank. But does it do the job? It certainly does perform by giving me wonderful leverage for removing and replacing. A friend of mine gave it to me some years ago and I really treasure it.

I have already mentioned pliers related to cones. We must not forget an assortment of pliers for other purposes. Here are a few examples: (1) Pointed or needlenosed (2) diagonal (3) cable-cutter.

CABLE CUTTERS   Obtain a good pair. I know that this tool together with the next one on the list are not really pliers, but nevertheless I am grouping them together. Next, you should have a good pair of powerful cutters. These are for cutting out old spokes, when rebuilding wheels. And last but not least, a pair of spoke end nippers. These are for cutting off any protruding spokes from the nipples after the wheel is built.

VICE GRIP Throughout THE BICYCLE MANUAL the reader will notice that I am referring constantly to our old friend the vise grip. You will find that these come in both straight and curved jaws. With care the curved type can be used on circular lock nuts, should you not have a "C" spanner.

TIN SNIPS These are used sometimes in conjunction with the hacksaw and are very useful for making liners, sleeves and ferrules.

STEEL BRUSH, CIRCULAR GRINDING WHEEL or EMERY WHEEL The well equipped workshop should have these tools. For the emery wheel a dressing tool is also essential. The operator should strive always to keep the wheel flat and in good condition. Nothing could look worse than a groove worn in the surface of the emery wheel.

GOGGLES Always wear goggles when you are grinding.

HAND WIRE BRUSHES These will be found most useful for those out-of-the-way places which are not always accessible to the fixed rotating brush.

ALLEN WRENCHES You should have both the standard and metric wrenches.

NUT DRIVERS They are indispensable for fender bolts and certain derailleur gear pivot nuts and bolts, to name just two of their many uses.

CROSS WRENCH For seats and saddles a cross wrench will come in very handy. You should have two of these, giving eight different sockets. Apart from getting the "hard-to-get-to-nuts" they possess more leverage than the ordinary nut drivers or socket wrenches. The last named should be in sizes (3/8"), (7/16"), (1/2") at the least, while 9-10-11-12 in metric make a useful companion to the tool chest or box.

RIVET EXTRACTOR   For chain installation we will need a rivet extractor—for 1/2" x 1/8" chains. But for the 3/32" derailleur chains, we need a pair of chain pliers. The reason for owning both is as follows: With the 1/8" chain a master link or spring link is used and is easily removed and replaced, whereas the derailleur chain has to be riveted. This is not always an easy task, remembering that it has to be done on the bicycle. The chain pliers will make this job very simple.

WHEEL BUILDING STAND   We must not forget a wheel building stand. If unobtainable we refer you to the chapter on wheel building, where you can see how to use an old fork for the job.

SPOKE NIPPLE KEYS   Of course we will need these. If possible get a circular type so that you can have several different sizes. Apart from the various gauges, a slight difference is sometimes found in the nipples of spokes of other manufacturers. For instance, the Japanese-made nipples, although of the same gauge are often a little larger than those from other countries.

FREEWHEEL CLUSTER REMOVERS   These should be varied as I have found three sizes of multi-splined clusters, while the two peg variety vary even more.

CHAIN STICK   This is a handy tool that can easily be made by the mechanic himself. I have made them with two lengths of chain, one side 1/8" and the other 3/32". These are used for removing cogs from threaded drivers or for changing cogs on clusters.

FORK STRAIGHTENER   This is the adjustable type for straightening the fork out of the bicycle.

FORK STRAIGHTENING JACK   This is for quick jobs, that is, for straightening the fork in the bicycle.

STRAIGHT EDGE   Do not forget the straight edge. We must have this tool when we wish to check the frame for alignment.

BICYCLE ERECTING STAND   This is a very important tool. If you want the very best get the Schwinn. It holds two bicycles and is adjustable in all ways. Once set to the tube diameter, the clamping lever is quick-release allowing for speedy installation and removal.

OXYACETYLENE WELDING KIT   For welding we will obviously need this kit and a good supply of rods, fluxes, mild steel and bronze rods. The latter, if possible, should be coated with flux—this facilitates the brazing job and saves the constant dipping of the rod into the flux.

COMPRESSOR   For tire inflation a fairly large compressor is desirable. With the appropriate end on the hose, you will find this very handy for blowing out dirt from awkward places on the bicycle. Likewise, when cleaning hub parts, etc., in the solvent tank, the surplus solvent can be blown off—this will speed the drying and cleaning.

SOLVENT TANK   The tank should be fitted with a pump. This will circulate the solvent through a filter so that the liquid can be used repeatedly before changing.

(TERMS)

ACTUATOR   A mechanical part which actuates forward drive. Example: the Bell Crank on a Shimano 3-speed hub.

ADJUSTER   The threaded barrel and lock-nut which controls the adjustment on the cables of brakes and gears.

ANGLES   When applied to a bicycle, this would refer to the head and seat angles of the frame.

ANNULUS or GEAR RING   The ring in a variable gear hub that usually has dogs to engage the clutch. It is furnished with spring-loaded pawls.

AXLE   A shaft or spindle on which a wheel or other rotating members are mounted. It can be either stationary or rotating, such as, chainwheels and cranks.

BALL-BEARINGS   Steel balls that are used for lessening friction in revolving parts. They can be fitted loose or mounted in cages or retainers, such as, in hubs, head sets and bottom bracket hangers.

BALLOON   A term used to denote large pneumatic tires. The 20 x 2.125 inch tire of a Sting-Ray bicycle is a good example.

BINDA   Racing handlebars that are named after the famous Italian Bicycling champion.

BINDER BOLT   A name used in the U.S.A. to describe the bolt which clamps the handlebar tight in the gooseneck. They are found either threaded into the stem or fitted with a nut.

BRACE   A thin strut of metal used to support enders.

BRAKE   Any of the devices used to retard a bicycle in motion. They can be either of the hand or foot variety.

BRAKE BLOCKS   These are manufactured from fibre and asbestos oblong blocks mounted in metal shoes, which when made to bear on the rim of the wheel will retard the bicycle.

BOLT   The threaded stud part of a nut and bolt. Some

people often mix up these two items.

BOTTOM BRACKET HANGER The short horizontal tube in which are contained the cups, axle and bearings that support the chainwheel and cranks. It is located at the junction of seat and down tubes and also the chain stays.

BURR A roughness or rough edge left on metal either in casting or cutting.

CABLE Originally named "Bowden Cable" after its inventor. It is a multi-stranded flexible wire contained within a housing for controlling cable brakes and variable gears.

CAGE The two metal plates holding the rollers of a derailleur gear. It also holds the guide on the front changer for switching the chain from one chainwheel to the other.

CALIPER A name given to the cable hand brake that suggests the engineers's measuring device.

CANNALURE A circular groove or fluting.

CENTER-PULL BRAKE A brake having equal pull on each side owing to the cable being attached to the center of the mechanism.

CHAIN The method of transmission in a bicycle that consists of a series of articulated links connected from the rear sprocket to front chainwheel.

CHAIN STAYS The tapered steel tubes that connect bottom-bracket to rear fork ends.

CHAIN WHEEL or FRONT SPROCKET The forward toothed wheel or wheels attached to the crank for propelling the bicycle.

CLUTCH A device for coupling two working parts. Example: the sliding clutch in a variable speed hub.

COASTER BRAKE A form of brake contained within the rear hub and actuated by backward pressure on the pedals.

CORE The insert to a Schrader valve which allows air to be pumped in and traps it inside the tube until its release is desirable.

COTTERLESS BRACKET   When the bicycle did away with pins for locking the hanger cups, they became known as having cotterless brackets.

COTTERLESS CRANKS   Cranks held to the bottom bracket axle without cotter pins. The method of attachment is usually by a splined or tapered square section to the end of the axle. A hex head bolt usually completes the locking arrangement.

COTTER PIN   A tapered threaded pin for holding crank to axle. In the past they were also used as a locking device for the bottom bracket cups.

CRANKS   Metal arms into one end of which are threaded the pedals. The other end being connected through or to the front sprocket. Made of steel or alluminum alloy, they are measured center to center.

CROWN RACE   The bottom cup or cone of the head set which rests on the fork crown.

CYCLOMETER   An instrument fitted to the front wheel for measuring miles traveled.

DERAILLEUR   A term derived from the French which means to derail or change the chain from one cog to another.

DISHING   A method of building a multi-sprocket equipped rear wheel so that the rim is central over the outer cone lock nuts. In a front wheel the rim is centered over the hub flanges, unless a cyclometer or such is fitted.

DOWN TUBE   The tube which connects the bottom of the head tube to the bottom bracket hanger.

DROPOUT   Refers to the rear diagonal fork ends of a bicycle as opposed to track ends.

DROPS   Racing style handle bars are often referred to simply as "drops."

DUST CAP   These are used on various components through-out the bicycle, such as, on the ends of pedals, over the ends of hubs and on the ends of inner tube valves.

FENDER or MUDGUARD   Metal or plastic coverings for the wheels to protect the rider from mud splashes when riding in the rain.

FERRULE   A bushing or thimble used variously to denote: (1) A sleeve to increase the diameter of the handlebar where it fits into the gooseneck. (2) The brake cablestop (also known as end button).

FRAME   The main tubular assembly that contains the bottom-bracket, the seat, the rear wheel, the front fork, the wheel assembly and handlebars.

FREEWHEEL   The toothed assembly consisting of one to six cogs which screws onto the rear hub and provides transmission by means of the chain to the front chainwheel. It is equipped with pawls and a ratchet allowing forward drive or coasting.

FRONT FORK   The member of the bicycle that is used for steering and holding of the front wheel. It consists of the column which swivels in the main frame and to which is attached the handlebars for steering. The blades which hold the front wheel are joined to the column by the fork crown.

FULCRUM   In a bicycle this usually refers to the clip and sleeve that supports the end of the outer casing of the three-speed cable when used with a pulley.

GEAR   In a bicycle this can mean the whole of the variable gear whether hub or of derailleur type. It can also refer to just the gear mechanism. A rider will also refer to which gear the bicycle is in, such as, in top, medium, or bottom gear.

GOOSENECK   (Stem or Extension) The tubular member usually shaped the numeral seven. It holds the handlebar to the front fork.

GREASE A thick oily or unctuous substance used as lubrication whereever bearings are present throughout the cycle.

HANDLEBAR The tubular member by which the bicycle is steered.

HEADSET The assembly consisting of cups, cones, balls and lock-nut which allows the fork to swivel in the frame.

HEAD TUBE The short upright tube into which is fitted the front fork via the head set. It is connected to the top and down tubes.

HEX HEAD BOLT A bolt that has a hexagonal head as opposed to a round raised or a head slotted for a screwdriver.

HOUSING Another name for the outer casing of the brake or gear cables. It is also used to denote the part of the brake lever assembly in which the lever proper pivots.

HUB The center part of a wheel in which is contained the axle cones and balls (A wheel minus spokes and rim).

KICKSTAND A propstand actuated by the foot for propping up the bicycle. Normally it would be situated just behind the bottom-bracket. It either bolts on or fits into a housing welded to the frame. The last named is a special feature of the Schwinn bicycle.

PEAR SHAPED The shape of the nipple on the end of a brake cable wire as used in hooded levers. The other type is known as a drum shape.

PEDALS The members that thread into the ends of the cranks for the feet to rest on when propelling the bicycle.

PINION Little cog wheels that rotate around the sun pinion and are installed in the planet cage of a variable speed hub.

PIVOT BOLT The center bolt on which the two arms of a caliper brake pivot.

PLUG This normally refers to the end plugs which seals up the handlebar end after taping.

POST   The piece of tubing on to which the seat clamps. It is also known as seat pillar, seat mast and seat pin.

PRESTA VALVE   The narrow type valve used in sew-up tires and some high pressure tubes.

PUMP or INFLATOR   An appliance for putting air into the tires.

"QUICK-RELEASE" in HUBS   A device consisting of a spring loaded skewer and cam mounted within the hollow hub axle which enables the wheels to be removed and replaced with alacrity. In brakes it is a cam lever, which when operated, opens the brake wider to assist further for speedy wheel removal.

RAT TRAP PEDALS   All metal pedals as opposed to pedals with rubber treads.

RIM   The outside metal part of a wheel, less hub, spokes and tire.

SCHRADER VALVE   The type of inner tube valve that is mostly used on bicycles in the U.S.A. It has a detachable core, but requires some effort when used with a hand pump for tube inflating.

SEAT CLUSTER   The junction of the frame where the seat and down tubes meet and are supported by the seat stays. It also receives the seat post and is equipped with a nut and bolt to clamp the post into the desired position.

SEAT POST   See post.

SEAT SADDLE   The leather or vinyl pad on which the rider sits.

SEAT STAYS   The thin tubes that connect the seat cluster to the bottom brakcet.

SEAT TUBE   The frame tube that connects the seat cluster to the bottom bracket.

SECONDARY CABLE   The short extra wire that connects the two arms of a center-pull brake and to which is added the anchor assembly for securing the main cable.

SHIMS   Thin washers that fit into a freewheel cluster to adjust the amount of play. It is sometimes ued to denote thin linings for packing handlebars and goosenecks.

SHOES   The metal holders into which the brake blocks are fitted. In some cases the metal retarders in these coaster brake hubs are referred to as shoes.

SPANNER   Another name for a wrench.

SPOKE   Thin wires that are laced into the hub to support the rim.

SPROCKET   A loosely used term for the front and rear toothed rings. A cog.

STEERING HEAD   See head tube and head set.

STEM   See gooseneck.

TAPE   Wrapping for the handlebar that is usually made of plastic or cotton twill.

TENSION ROLLER   The lower roller in the derailleur cage which tensions the chain. The upper roller which guides the chain is usually known as the jockey roller.

TIRES (Tubular)   Ultra-lightweight racing tires with the inner tubes contained inside the casing by sewing the edges together on the inside circumference.

TIRES (Wired-on)   Tires with the inner tubes seperate from the outer cover.

TOE CLIPS   Metal cages that are generally equipped with straps fitted to the forward part of the pedals. They are used to assist the rider's pedalling action.

TOP TUBE   The member of the frame that connects the head tube to seat tube cluster.

VALVE   See Presta and Schrader.

VARIABLE GEARED   Defines a bicycle that is equipped with more than one gear ratio. Example: Three, four or five-speed hub. Or three through fifteen-speeds with derailleur gears.

WOODS VALVE   Type of valve that relies on rubber sleeving to trap the air in the tube. It also makes for easy hand pumping.

Because of the great popularity of cycling in America, several European manufacturing companies have either made their range of tools available or have produced new tools for the bicycle industry in this country.

Besides such firms as Var of France and Campagnolo of Italy with their fine line of tools there is an American company, Park Tool of St. Paul, Minnesota, who also make an excellent line of tools. We recommend that the reader send for their current catalog.

BIBLIOGRAPHY

Bartleet, *H.W. Bartleet's Bicycle Book*. London: Ed. J. Burrow and Company. 1931.

Cycling. *Merit Badge Series Publication:* *Boy Scouts of America*. 1970

Cycling Book of Maintenance. London: Temple Press Books, Ltd. 1961.

Gear Ratios. Cyclo-Gear Co. Ltd.

Reynold's "531" Cycle Tubing: Reynold's Tube Co. Ltd.

Shaw, *R.C. Teach Yourself Cycling*. London: The English Universities Press, Ltd. 1963.

A special thanks to my wife Marie, our children Roger, Rosie, the twins Barbara and Heather for their encouragement and patience during the many months it took for me to complete the manuscript of THE BICYCLE MANUAL.

—R. W.

ACKNOWLEDGEMENTS

Arthur J. Simas, *Safety Cycle Shop*, Los Angeles, California; *Schwinn Bicycle Co.;* Chicago, Illinois; *Raleigh Industries*, Long Beach, Ca.; *Columbia Manufacturing Co.*, Westerfield, Mass.; *Euro-Imports*, Los Angeles, Ca., *Andreis & K T M; United Imports,* Gardena, Ca., *Peugeout & Steyr*; *West Coast Cycle Supply*, Nishiki; *Wheel Goods*, Minneapolis, Minn.; *Big Wheel, Ltd.*, Denver, Colo.; *Bicycle Institute of America*, New York, N.Y.

The Bendix Co., U.S.A.; *Goodyear Tire & Rubber Co.,* U.S.A.; *Cyclist's Touring Club*, Godalming, Surrey, England; *Clement Co.*, Italy; *Bianchi Co.*, Italy; *Campagnola Co.*, Italy; *Weinman Co.*, Switzerland; *Huret Co.*, France; *Mafac Co.*, France; *Simplex Co.*, France; *Le Cycliste*, Paris, France.

John A. Volpe, Secretary of Transportation, Washington D.C.; Herbert F. Simone, Assistant Secretary for Environment and Urban Systems, Washington D.C.; Asa Warren, Glendora, Ca., Western Regional Director, American Youth Hostels, Inc.

Walter Hurst, George and Shirley Arraj; and Evalyn Smylie,

ROBERT WHITER
CYCLES
Wood Green
London . N22

Now Residing In Los Angeles, California

A.I.Cyc.T.

Associate of the Incorporated
Institute of Cycle Traders and Repairers.

Facsimile of Robert Whiter's Cycle decal crest. This went on
the front of every cycle frame he made.